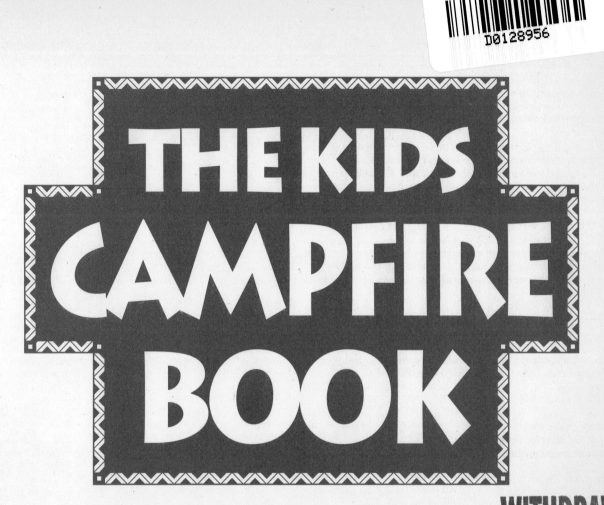

THE KIDS CAMPFIRE BOOK

BY JANE DRAKE & ANN LOVE **WITHDRAWN**

ILLUSTRATED BY HEATHER COLLINS

SONGS ARRANGED BY MATTHEW DEWAR

KIDS CAN PRESS

Published in Canada by
Kids Can Press Ltd.
29 Birch Avenue
Toronto, Ontario M4V 1E2

Published in the U.S. by
Kids Can Press Ltd.
85 River Rock Drive, Suite 202
Buffalo, NY 14207

Edited by Laurie Wark
Designed by Blair Kerrigan/Glyphics
Printed and bound in Canada by Kromar Printing Ltd.

US 98 0 9 8 7 6 5 4 3 2

US PA 98 0 9 8 7 6 5 4 3 2

Canadian Cataloguing in Publication Data

Drake, Jane
 The kids campfire book

1st U.S. ed.
ISBN 1-55074-454-2 (bound)   ISBN 1-55074-539-5 (pbk.)

1. Campfire programs – Juvenile literature. 2. Outdoor
recreation – Juvenile literature. 3. Amusements –
Juvenile literature. I. Collins, Heather. II. Love,
Ann. III. Title.

GV198.R4D73 1998   j796.54'5   C97-931953-6

This book is dedicated to
our families,
with whom we have shared
our campfire evenings.

CONTENTS

THE SPARK

THE BLAZE

ACKNOWLEDGMENTS

Henry and Kay Barnett; Ian, Judy, Andrea, Brianna, Natalie and Hilary Barnett; Will, Fran, Greg and Patrick Barnett; Vic and Barbara Barnett; Doreen Barnett; Joyce Barnett; Betsy Bascom; Cathi Bremner; Trish Brooks; Nancy and Renny Cannon; Jennifer Cayley; Jane Crist; Rick Davidson; Jim, Stephanie, Brian and Madeline Drake; Ruth and Charlie Drake; Tom, Cindy, Patricia, James and Emily Drake; Jayne Frye; Charles Gall, SOCAN; Girl Guides of Canada; Jennie Gruss; Ethan and Mryka Hall-Beyer; Christine Hedden; Terry Horgan; Julie Hunt-Correa; Judy Lank; David Latimer and Kilcoo Camp; Matt Lato; Kathleen and Donald Leitch; Susan Leppington; Mary Ann and Rob Lewis; Jim Lisowski; David, Melanie, Jennifer and Adrian Love; Peter, Charmian, Colin, Gage, Gaelin and Alison Love, and Melanie Manchee; Betty and Gage Love; Patricia McGillivary; Dr. McGuigin, HSC Poison Control Centre; John, Marleen, Amy and Carey Morgan; Phil Mozel; Donna O'Connor; Peninsula Pharmacy; Hilary Robinson; Esther and Mike Robson; Yvonne and Jack Sellers; Stephanie Smith; Barb and Jack Spitler; Doug Stewart; Ruth and Walt Stewart; Dennis Stitt; Margie Stockwell-Hart; Camp Tanamakoon; Mary Thompson; Derek Totten; Russell Usher; Elizabeth Vosburgh; Herb and Dorothy Wyngard.

The final acknowledgment can be sung to the tune of "Fire's Burning" (see page 97).

Thanks to Valerie and Ricky
Matt, Laurie and Janine
Heather and Blair
And the staff at Kids Can.

For the non-singers in the crowd, the authors gratefully acknowledge the tremendous support and shared expertise of Valerie Hussey, Ricky Englander, Janine Belzak and all the people on the Kids Can Press team. A special thanks to our editor, Laurie Wark, who remains organized and focused despite the demands of new motherhood. We are pleased to be working once more with Heather Collins as illustrator and Blair Kerrigan as designer. And we welcome a new voice with this book — musician and song arranger Matt Dewar.

INTRODUCTION

A campfire evening glows and fades with the life of the fire. First you have the fun of getting ready — gathering wood, food, friends and family. Excitement mounts as the spark is lit. By the time the fire bursts into a strong blaze, everyone is telling stories, singing old favorites and playing crazy games. When the blaze settles into hot coals, the fire is perfect for cooking. As the coals soften into glowing embers and strange sounds come from the dark, the mood is set for telling ghost stories. Finally, a happy quiet falls over the campfire and someone yawns. It's time to put out the fire and snuggle down for a peaceful sleep.

As the campfire moves along, so does this book — from the gathering of fuel and friends, through the first spark, the strong blaze, the hot coals, then the last embers. You will discover how to tend the fire at each stage, and you'll find night adventures, good eating, fun games and stories along the way. Choose songs from the music section at the end of the book to fit the mood and to add the special feeling that singing gives a campfire evening.

Caution: In some communities and at certain times of the year, open fires are not permitted or need a license. Check at your local police or government offices if you are unsure of the regulations in your area.

Always have an adult around whenever a campfire is lit.

THE SPARK

This section gives you some tips on choosing the best kind of wood for a successful campfire, placing the fire so no one will be bothered by smoke or mosquitoes, making sure-fire firestarters, constructing sturdy log seats, making bonfire utensils and lots more.

When fuel, food and friends are gathered, it is time to start the fire. Read on to find out how to light the tinder, keep that spark alive and turn it into a strong bonfire or cooking fire. Try a few campfire games and look out for some natural "sparks" and "fires" in the dusk beyond the flames.

THE RIGHT SITE

Choose your campfire site during the day when you can check out the whole area. Follow these tips to find a spot that is fun, safe and bug free.

- Look for an open area. It is unsafe to light a fire near or under trees or bushes because rising sparks can set branches on fire. Your fire will be no bigger around than a bicycle tire, but you will need space around it for people to stoke the fire, cook, bring in more wood and just sit to enjoy the blaze. A sandy beach or a rocky point jutting out into a lake are ideal campfire sites.

- Check that sparks won't drift from your site toward anything that will burn. Toss a piece of light, dry grass or birch bark into the breeze and watch in which direction it is carried to be sure nothing burnable lies in the way. If it's really windy, don't light a fire at all, but wait for a calmer evening.

- Clear a circle 3 m (10 ft.) back from the center of the fire site right down to bare soil or rock. Remove all twigs, bark, needles, leaves, grass, moss and anything else that might burn.

- Dig down 5 cm (2 in.) into the soil at the center of your cleared site and check for roots. Fire can spread underground along roots and set nearby trees ablaze. Then, pack the soil back down hard with your hands and feet. This will be the base of your fire pit.

◆ Don't build a rock circle around the fire. Rock heats up to high temperatures near a fire and can crack or even explode — especially if the rock is wet.

◆ To avoid mosquitoes, site your fire away from places where they breed — still water, marshy areas and bogs. Also, keep away from valley bottoms or hollows where there is no air movement. Sites at the edge of a lake will usually have a gentle breeze to blow away annoying bugs and smoke too.

◆ Always keep a pail of water, a large bucket of sand and a shovel near the fire. Just one spark, a gust of wind, some dry leaves, and your campfire can flare up and start a larger fire. A small fire can be put out with water. Use the shovel to throw sand on any runaway flames to smother them. Make sure you get adult help immediately and call for the fire department if the fire gets out of control.

MAKE A WOODPILE

A good woodpile is a handy source of dry wood for adding to the blaze and keeps spare wood safely away from the fire. Here's how to organize one:

1. Find a place a short walk from the fire where the wind will not drop sparks. A spot sheltered by trees or overhanging rocks will help keep the wood dry.

2. Lay two long sticks, about as thick as an arm, on the ground. This base will keep your firewood off the damp earth.

3. Pile the wood across the sticks with bigger fuel logs together at one end, mid-sized pieces in the center and smaller sticks for starting the fire at the other end.

TELLING THE WOODS FROM THE TREES

When you are searching for firewood, look for dry deadfall or driftwood, not live wood. If you roll over a log and a salamander wriggles away, gently roll the log back. If a salamander likes the log, it will be too damp for firewood.

It's a good idea to decide what kind of campfire you want before collecting your wood. A fire that is best for cooking needs different kinds of wood than a fire started for heat.

HARDWOOD OR SOFTWOOD?

Stand at almost any forest edge and you will likely see two kinds of trees — evergreen and deciduous. Evergreen trees usually have the needle-like leaves that stay green year-round. Deciduous trees have regular, flat leaves that drop off in autumn.

Deciduous trees grow more slowly than evergreens and have heavier, firmer wood. That is why foresters call deciduous trees hardwood and evergreen trees softwood. Softwood burns quickly, lets off lots of heat and dies leaving no coals. It makes a colorful bonfire — but you need plenty of it for a whole evening. Hardwood takes longer to catch, burns slowly and turns to glowing coals, so it's perfect for a cooking fire.

When you're looking for firewood, it's hard to tell whether a stick on the ground comes from a softwood or hardwood tree. Stop and look around for clues. The stick likely fell from a nearby tree and there may be more sticks with bark or leaves attached.

Remember, good firewood is dry. Rotten or crumbly wood, wet wood or wood so green it bends without cracking will make a smoky fire. Poplar can smoke even when it is dry. Avoid softwood with balls of tree gum attached and the fire will not spit as much.

HERE ARE GOOD-BURNING HARDWOOD AND SOFTWOOD TREES TO WATCH FOR:

HARDWOOD

maple
gray or reddish brown bark

ash
dark brown, furrowed and scaly bark

beech
smooth gray bark and saw-toothed leaves

oak
watch for nearby acorns

birch
peeling, white bark with black patches

hickory
watch for the nut husk that splits open into four sections

SOFTWOOD

spruce
short, spiky needles encircle the twigs

pine
long needles in groups of two, three or five

cedar
flat needles fan in a long, lacy spray

hemlock and **fir**
short, flattened needles twist along twigs

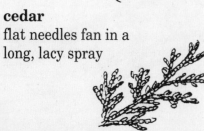

POISON IVY AND POISON OAK

Never collect wood near Poison Ivy or Poison Oak. Touching the leaves can give you a serious rash. The smoke from burning any part of the plants can also give you a rash.

The leaves of these plants grow in groups of three. The plants may be small with just three leaves on one stem or bushy with many leaves growing in groups of three. The leaves are shiny green in spring and turn reddish in fall. Sometimes the plants have white or light yellow berries.

**Leaflets three,
leave them be;
Berries white, shun
the sight!**

13

COLLECTING WOOD

When you are collecting wood for a campfire, look for tinder and kindling to get the fire going and then bigger logs to fuel the blaze.

TINDER

Tinder is fine, dry material that catches easily with a match and bursts into flame. Many people use small balls of newspaper for tinder. In a meadow, collect weed tops from last year's asters, milkweed, goldenrod or cattails. Near a forest, collect tiny pieces of dead twigs, dry pine cones, pine needles and fallen birch bark. Remember never to peel bark off a live tree.

KINDLING

You will need at least two big handfuls of kindling wood to keep the flame alive. Kindling must be so dry it snaps when broken. Look for the dead lower branches of a softwood tree because they are usually drier than sticks lying on the ground. Do not rip the dead twigs off too close to the trunk or the live parts of the tree may be damaged.

FUEL

Fuel is the wood that keeps the fire burning. You will need at least two big armfuls of fuel for a campfire evening. All fuelwood should be as dry as possible. Look for pieces about as thick as your thigh.

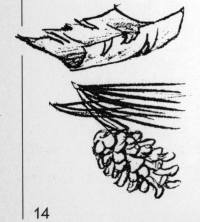

14

SWEATSHIRT WOOD CARRIER

Gathering wood for a fire is easy with an old sweatshirt or long-sleeved shirt.

1.
Lay the shirt on the ground with the arms and body spread out flat.

2.
Place collected sticks up and down on the body section until you have two good armloads of wood.

3.
Cross the sleeves tightly and tie them in a square knot over the sticks as shown.

4.
Swing the bundle over your shoulder so the knot touches your back. Keep one sleeve over one shoulder and pull the other sleeve under your other arm. Tie the sleeves across your chest.

5.
Now you can walk with your arms free to collect more wood as you go.

HOMEMADE FIRESTARTERS

Wood holds wetness for a long time, so it's good to have waxed firestarters handy in case your kindling won't catch. You can make firestarters in the kitchen with leftover candles and wax crayons. Store them in a container until it is time to light a fire.

First, have an adult help you prepare the melted wax.

You'll need:

a clean, empty can (such as a coffee or soup can)
leftover crayons and candle stubs
a cooking pot
a pot holder

1.
Fill the can half full with crayon and candle stubs. Place the can inside the pot.

2.
Pour water into the cooking pot (not the can), keeping the water level halfway up the side of the can. If the can floats, pour some of the water out of the pot until the can rests on the bottom.

3.
Have an adult place the pot on a stove element. Turn the element on low and wait for the wax to melt.

4.
Have an adult turn off the stove and remove the pot. Once it's cool, lift the can of melted wax out of the pot and place it on a pot holder or hotplate. Now you're ready to make the waxed firestarters on these pages.

FIRE PARCELS

You'll need:

melted wax
newspaper
string
scissors

1.
Roll several sheets of newspaper lengthwise tightly. Tie big bows of string every few centimeters (inches) along the length.

FIRE CUBES

WAXED MATCHES

2.
Cut the newspaper roll between the string ties to form little packets of paper.

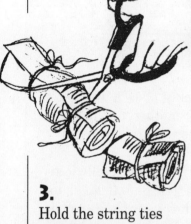

You'll need:
melted wax
an empty cardboard egg carton
scissors
string
a handful of sawdust or wood chips

1.
Cut or rip the lid off the egg carton.

2.
Place a piece of string in each cup of the cardboard carton, leaving one end to dangle over the side of the cup.

3.
Fill the cups with sawdust or wood chips.

4.
Pour the melted wax into each cup and let it cool.

5.
Separate the cups of the egg carton by ripping or cutting in between them.

3.
Hold the string ties and dip the packets of newspaper into the wax. Lay the waxed packets on unused newspaper to cool.

When these waxed matches are lit, they burn longer than regular matches, and are waterproof too!

You'll need:
melted wax
string
wooden matches
kitchen tongs
newspapers

1.
Wrap a piece of string tightly around a wooden matchstick, but do not cover the tip.

2.
With kitchen tongs, dip the whole match, tip and all, in melted wax. Let it cool on newspaper. Strike the match as usual to light it.

LIGHTING THE FIRE

Now that you've found the perfect site and gathered your wood, family and friends . . . it's time to build the fire and light it!

Kneel facing the fire pit with your back to the breeze. Lay two pieces of kindling in the center of the fire pit so they form an angle opening toward you. Pile some tinder in the kindling. The tinder should be compact enough that the pieces are all touching each other, but loose enough that it remains light and full of air.

Use a wooden match if possible. Strike the match and tip it slightly down so the flame catches onto the wood of the matchstick. If there is a breeze, cup your hands around the flame to protect it. When it is well lit, push the matchstick into the center of the tinder. Blow gently into the base of the fire pit for the flame to catch. If the tinder does not flame quickly, place a firestarter (see page 16) in it and try another match. When the tinder catches, add more until you have a good, strong flame.

Once the tinder is burning, add small pieces of kindling, one piece at a time, in a tepee shape around the flame. Place the pieces close enough together so they catch fire from each other, but leave little air spaces between them so the fire can breathe. Build the tepee gradually, adding slightly larger sticks each time. Once the larger pieces of kindling are burning well, it's time to shape the fire into a campfire for heat or for cooking.

DOUBLE-CHECK FOR SAFETY

◆ Be sure an adult is nearby and knows you are starting the campfire.
◆ Have a shovel and pails of water and sand nearby (see page 11).
◆ Be sure it is not windy. It is also wise to know the direction of the breeze (see page 10).
◆ Anyone tending the fire should tie back loose hair and tuck in loose clothing.
◆ Never leave the fire unattended.

A CAMPFIRE FOR HEAT

When the kindling is burning steadily, gradually add larger pieces of softwood fuel to the fire, keeping the tepee shape. If the main fuel logs are as big around as two hands can circle, then build up the fire until three are burning well at one time. A fire needs three good logs burning together to throw off heat. More than five logs and the fire gets too large and hot. Add a new log whenever one of the three main logs burns down to the size of a piece of kindling.

When the fire is going well, the kindling tepee will probably collapse into a crisscross formation in the fire pit. Use a fire poker to push the logs together after a collapse. Add fresh logs across the top because fire burns upward.

A COOKING FIRE

Using hardwood only, add small logs to the kindling tepee, until three are burning well. When the tepee collapses, poke the logs so the butt ends — the cut ends — all lie facing the breeze and the lengths of the logs lie along the line of the breeze. After about an hour of stoking, the fire should have plenty of glowing coals. The fire is now ready for cooking in the coals (see page 58).

(see page 58).

FIRE CIRCLE CEREMONY

Once the kindling is burning well, invite each friend to add a piece of fuel to the fire. As they do this, they can introduce themselves and make a wish or say what the best — or the worst — part of their day was. This ceremony is a good way to welcome guests and get everyone started on an evening of storytelling, singing and fun.

19

CAMPFIRE GIZMOS AND GADGETS

Once you've started a tradition of campfire evenings, you'll want to create a few accessories so that firemaking is easy and safe. You'll need a poker, a chopping block and a stone pot rest.

FIRE POKER

A properly tended fire needs several good pokes throughout the evening. As the logs burn down, nudge them closer so they'll keep burning. Make a poker from green hardwood, so it won't catch fire or hold on to sparks. Trim the twigs and leaves off a 1 m (3 ft.) poker stick. Choose a place to keep it where it won't be added to the fire by mistake.

CHOPPING BLOCK

When a neighbor or your family chops down a dead tree, save a large, flat slice for a chopping block. The block provides a sturdy, flat surface for splitting wood. Make sure it's placed where it won't catch fire.

STONE POT REST

Don't wait until the food is boiling over to look for a pot rest — it's better to plan ahead. Scout around a beach or field for a rock that is flat and big enough to hold a large cooking pot. Place this rock about 1 m (3 ft.) from the fire. Then you can transfer a pot from the fire to a safe and flat place. You'll need kitchen pot holders to protect your hands too.

KNIFE AND HATCHET SAFETY

A good knife or penknife and a hatchet are essential tools for setting a fire, but it takes careful practice with an adult to learn to use them properly.

- Always cut with the blade going away from your body.

- Remember, knives are tools, not toys. Always handle them with care.

- Take care of the knife and hatchet by keeping them clean, dry and sharp. Sharpen them on a sharpening stone by using a drop of oil, such as WD-40, on the blade and stroke the blade away from your body at a 20-degree angle to the stone. Wipe off any excess oil with an old rag or newspaper. Keep the blades lightly oiled.

- Store the knife and hatchet away from younger children. Knives should be kept closed or in a sheath. Hatchets should be stored with the blade covered in a thick leather sheath.

CAMPFIRE FURNITURE

Make your campfire cozy with rustic handcrafted furniture. Bring along an old cushion or sleeping bag and you'll be all set for a fun evening.

STUMP STOOL

When your family or neighbors cut down a dead tree for firewood, set aside the larger logs for stump stools. Have an adult trim the logs so that they are level and about 50 cm (20 in.) high. You might want to smooth the top and edges of the stump with some sandpaper to remove any splinters or rough areas. You can even seal the top of your stool with a thin coat of water-based varnish to keep it from rotting in the rain.

CAMPFIRE CANDLES

Light the path to the campfire with candles glowing in paper bags. The bag keeps the wind off the flame and can be reused another night.

You'll need:
brown, flat-bottomed paper grocery bags
sand
candle stubs, at least 10 cm (4 in.) tall

1.
Fold down the top of each bag to form a 5 cm (2 in.) cuff on the outside of the bag.

2.
Moisten the sand with a little water so it is damp but not runny. Fill the bottom of each bag with 10 to 15 cm (4 to 6 in.) of sand. Place the bags every 2 m (6 1/2 ft.) along the path to the campfire.

3.
Place one candle stub securely in the sand in the middle of each bag.

4.
Have an adult help you light the candles. Throughout the evening, check the paper bag candles to make sure they are burning safely. They may burn out in the sand, but make sure they are out cold before you go to bed for the night. Until the next campfire, store the bags and candles in a shed or other waterproof place. Dampen the sand each time before reusing the bags.

LOG BENCHES

Two logs can be used to make a campfire bench. Site your bench so it's facing the water. The night breezes will blow the smoke toward the lake.

You'll need:

an adult helper

2 logs that are the same length but different thicknesses

a saw

scraps of wood the size of hockey sticks, or old tent pegs

a hatchet

a hammer

1.
Position the logs so that they lie parallel to each other and are at least 1 m (3 ft.) away from the fire. The thicker log should be farthest away from the fire, providing a back rest. The thinner log will be the seat.

2.
Have an adult saw wooden scraps into eight pieces — four about 30 cm (12 in.) long and four approximately 50 cm (20 in.) long. Make pegs by sharpening one end of each piece, using the hatchet.

3.
Hammer the smaller pegs into the ground in front of the seat log.

4.
Push the back-rest log up against the seat log and wedge it in place by hammering in the larger pegs very close to the log.

If you are making your log bench on rock or where the soil is too hard or thin for pegs, use heavy rocks to keep the bench in place.

23

CAMPFIRE COOKING UTENSILS

You don't have to be a scout to make campfire cooking utensils. But you do have to be able to identify trees. Many of the varieties that make poor fuel work well for utensils.

Birch is best for roasting sticks and is easily recognized by its white bark with black stripes. Young birch trees often have suckers or small branches growing at their base. When they are as big around as a fat pencil they make a perfect roasting stick. Alder, chokecherry and red dogwood are other varieties that make good cooking tools. They grow as shrubs, sometimes reaching tree size.

SAFETY ALERT

When you're looking for wood to make utensils, don't choose pine or other conifers — they have sap that can flare when it's heated. Also, if you are allergic to aspirin, do not use willow branches. Willows contain the natural ingredients found in the drug aspirin.

GREEN STICK GRILL

You'll need:

a birch branch or sucker, 1 m (3 ft.) long

a sharp penknife

1.
Choose a branch that is green and flexible. With an adult helper, slice it off close to the ground. If you use a sucker branch from the tree, slice it off cleanly without tearing the surrounding bark.

2.
Hold the fat end of the branch firmly in one hand and the penknife in the other. With the blade turned away from your body, carefully remove all the leaves and any small twigs. Leave the main branches intact, including the long, skinny tip.

3.
Bend the skinny end of the branch around to form an "0" or an oval. Secure it in place by tying the tip in several knots. You may want to have someone tie it while you hold the stick in place.

4.
Crisscross all smaller branches across the "0" and tie any loose ends to the outside of the "0." Weave in small twigs with their leaves and twigs removed to make a sturdy grill surface.

5.
For cooking on your stick grill, see page 60.

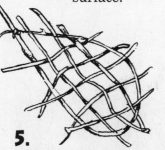

ROASTING STICK

You'll need:

a birch branch or sucker, 1 m (3 ft.) long

a sharp penknife

1.
Choose and trim a branch or sucker as you did for the Green Stick Grill.

2.
This time leave only one main branch intact. If your branch forks in two, you can make a double toasting stick.

3.
Sharpen the skinny end of the stick using small strokes of the penknife. Always stroke away from your body.

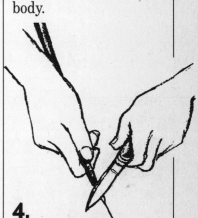

4.
Use your roasting stick to cook hot dogs or marshmallows. For cooking instructions, turn to pages 58 and 76.

25

POT HOOK

When the pot handle gets too hot to touch, reach for a handy pot hook. Then you can move the pot around on the grill or take the pot to your stone pot rest without scorching your fingers. You should use pot holders too.

You'll need:

2 V-shaped branches as big around as a broom handle, 40 cm (15 in.) long

a saw

heavy string, 1 m (3 ft.) long

1.
Trim the branches with the saw, making one side of the V longer on one branch.

2.
Line up the two branches as shown. Knot the string as tightly as possible around both branches so the string covers 8 cm (3 in.) of the two branches. Knot the loose end of string around the stick to hold it in place.

3.
Keep this pot hook ready for every cookout.

CHOOSING COOKING POTS

Stainless-steel pots make the best camping pots. They are lightweight and conduct heat well. Choose a pot that is sturdy but not too heavy. (Thin pots can bend and warp when they're used directly in a campfire.) Rub the outside bottom and sides of the pot with a bar of soap before you use it. This helps prevent the pot from becoming covered with soot and makes clean up easier.

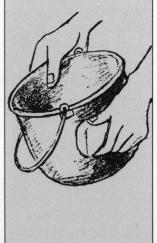

NIGHTWATCH

Animals of the night have big eyes and see better in the dark. Their eyes reflect the light they pick up, creating eyeshine. You can identify who is looking at you by the color of the eyeshine and the shape of the eyes.

looking down from a tree or moving above the ground, yellow eyes — raccoon

unblinking, green oval eyes — cat

bright white eyes — dog or coyote

on the ground, tiny, moving specks of white or ruby red — spider eyes

on the ground or in the water, small eyes shining green dots — bullfrog

27

BEAT THE BUGS

There are more than 7000 kinds of blackflies in North America, so no matter where you have your campfire, these pesky insects will likely find you. In pioneer times flies were so numerous that people tried everything to get rid of them. They even dried wolf and moose droppings and burned them in a can. The aroma seemed to keep the insects away — as well as the neighbors. Flies and mosquitoes still cause people to itch and swat every summer. Try some of the ideas on these pages to keep hungry insects away.

HOMEMADE SMUDGE POT

This smudge pot will help to discourage insects from visiting your campfire.

You'll need:
scissors
wicking or fine cotton string
a clean, empty soup can
2 short sticks
a small ball of modeling clay
a clean, empty coffee can
candle wax and/or candle stubs
a heavy pot
a pot holder
25 mL (2 tbsp.) citronella oil (available at a drugstore)

1.
Cut a piece of wicking or string to measure the same height as the soup can. Tie one end of the string to the middle of the stick. Attach the clay ball to the other end of the string.

2.
Fill the coffee can half full with candle stubs and candle wax. Place the can inside the cooking pot.

3.

Add water to the cooking pot (not the can), keeping the water level halfway up the side of the can. If the can floats, spoon some of the water out of the pot until the can rests on the bottom.

4.

Have an adult place the pot on a stove element. Turn the element on low and wait for the wax to melt.

5.

Have an adult turn off the stove and remove the pot from the heat. Lift the can of melted wax out of the pot and place it on a pot holder, hotplate or a protected table.

6.

Add citronella oil to the melted wax and stir the mixture gently with a stick. Carefully fill the soup can with this mixture to just below the rim of the can. *Caution: Citronella should be used with adult supervision. It is not a food. It tastes very bitter and can cause stomach aches if it is swallowed.*

7.

Drop the clay ball and string into the middle of the soup can and rest the stick across the top of the can. Allow the citronella smudge pot to cool and harden.

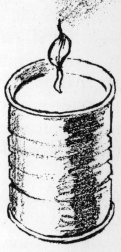

Why not make several smudge pots? Light them at the beginning of each campfire evening and blow them out at the end.

THE BUZZ ON AVOIDING MOSQUITOES

- Wear light-colored clothes. Mosquitoes like dark colors, especially blue. A long-sleeved shirt and long pants will help keep mosquitoes off your skin.

- Take a swim before spending the evening outside. Mosquitoes swarm around sweaty people.

- Apply citronella or repellent *before* making banana boats for dessert (recipe on page 77). Mosquitoes are attracted to bananas.

- Relax. Mosquitoes are attracted to nervous or worried people.

FIREFLY CHAT

On a warm summer evening, look away from the campfire toward a grassy area. You may see the blinking light of a firefly in the dark. The firefly may blink a signal several times in the same rhythm. With a flashlight and a little know-how, you can carry on a conversation with a firefly and lure it closer for a good look.

TALK WITH A FIREFLY

There are more than fifty species of fireflies (or lightning bugs) in North America, and each kind has its own unique signal. A signal has a series of light flashes, sent in a specific rhythm. These signals are used to attract a mate. Male fireflies usually flash their signals as they fly, but females signal while resting on a leaf or a blade of grass. After mating, the female lays her eggs on damp soil or a rotting log, and both adults die. In one kind of firefly, the female will attract a male and mate; but then she will send out a false message and attract a male of a different firefly species so she can eat him.

Watch for a firefly blinking on a summer evening. Try to count the number of flashes in its signal. There could be three, four or up to seven. Note the rhythm between individual blinks and between whole signals. Then, decide if the firefly is female or male by whether the light is in one place or moving.

If it is male (moving), be a female by holding a flashlight in one spot and mimicking the signal back. With luck, the male will fly up to you, thinking you are a mate.

FIREFLY LANTERN

Before the time of electricity, people in Japan and China collected fireflies and put them in paper lanterns. If enough fireflies were caught, their constant flashings gave off a pretty glow. The light did not last long, however, because fireflies live as adults for little more than a week.

If you catch a firefly, put it in a clean jar and cover it with your hand. After watching the firefly for a few minutes, let it go. North American fireflies will die if they're left long in a container, even with air holes punched in the top. A free firefly can mate, lay its eggs and make more fireflies for next year.

BIOLUMINESCENT BUGS

Firefly light is made by a chemical reaction in the insect's tail. Light produced this way, inside a living plant or animal, is called bioluminescence. Adult fireflies blink, or turn on and off their bioluminescence, but firefly eggs and worms glow all over with a fainter, steady light. Other North American insects that glow with bioluminescence are the fire beetle and the glow-worm beetle.

Sometimes people claim they have seen a bioluminescent frog. After a closer look, they find it's not the frog that is glowing. The many fireflies the frog ate are glowing in its stomach through its transparent skin.

CAMPFIRE GAMES

The fire is crackling and the smudge pot is burning, so now it's the time for fun and games.

TELEPHONE

Everyone sits in a circle around or near the fire. The youngest person starts the game by whispering a message in the ear of the person on her right. She might say a tongue twister or something simple, such as "Dad cooks great burgers" or "Mary mixes marvelous milk shakes." The message is passed from ear to ear until the last person repeats what he's been told. You'll be in stitches when you hear "Cool Dad eats bridges" or "Mash mealy muffins, Mary."

CAMPFIRE TELEPHONE

Everyone sitting in the campfire circle joins hands. The person with a birthday closest to July 1 starts the game by squeezing a message to the person seated on his right. It can be an ordinary squeeze, or a series of squeezes like Morse code. The message travels around the circle until it comes back to the start. See how much the message changes. Try to do it quickly so that the message flashes around the circle in the shortest time possible.

THE CAMPFIRE WAVE

If you have a big group sitting around the campfire, try doing the campfire wave. Pick the oldest person to go first. She stands up and raises her hands over her head, lowers her hands and then sits down. The person beside her starts to stand up when she is raising her hands, followed by the next person and so on. It's fun to start out slowly, then keep going around the circle faster and faster until everyone collapses — laughing and exhausted.

RAINMAKER

If it's been a hot day and you need cooling off, try rainmaking. One person begins and is joined by the person on her right and so on until the action travels all the way around the circle. The noise gets louder as each person in the circle joins in. Then the first person will do the next action and it will travel around the circle.

ROUND 1
Rub your hands together so they make a swishing noise.

ROUND 2
Snap the fingers of both hands, moving your arms up and down, while making a popping sound with your tongue on the roof of your mouth. It sounds like water falling to the ground.

ROUND 3
Slap hands on your knees. The rain is really splashing down.

ROUND 4
Pound the ground with fists or palms. The storm is at its height.

ROUND 5
Slap hands on your knees more quietly.

ROUND 6
Snap fingers very gently.

ROUND 7
Rub hands forward and back, pressing lightly.

Sit still and listen. The storm has passed — do you feel cooler?

33

CAMPFIRE GAMES WITH A BEAT

Now it's time to pick up the pace and shake those bodies with these peppy campfire games.

LET ME SEE YOUR PINK FLAMINGO

Before you begin this chanting game, think up as many animal actions as possible. They can be simple or silly, such as itchy monkey *(scratching head and underarm)*, dancing chicken *(flapping wings and strutting)*, funky turtle *(neck in and out of a shell)* and fluttering butterfly *(dance around flapping arms up and down)*.

Divide the group in two and stand on each side of the campfire, leaving space between each person to do the actions.

Group 1 says, "Let me see your pink flamingo!"

Group 2 says, "What's that you say?"

Group 1 shouts louder, "I said, let me see your pink flamingo!"

Group 2 demonstrates its pink flamingo *(stand on one leg and waggle your long neck)*

Group 1 chants, "Ooh, ahh, pink flamingo, ooh, ahh, one more time" — *group 2 does its pink flamingo again* — "ooh, ahh, pink flamingo, ooh, ahh, get back in line."

Now the second group chants to the first group, "Let me see your itchy monkey," and so on. After playing this game several times you'll discover family or group favorites. You might even find a comedian in the crowd.

LET'S GET THE RHYTHM

This is another chanting game that gets you knee-slapping with the beat. Each person is given a number — if there are five people, use five numbers from 0 to 8, leaving some unused ghost numbers for added fun and confusion. The 0 person goes first after everyone chants the chorus.

Chorus: *(do the actions as you chant the words, except where there is only clapping)*

Let's get *(slap knees twice)* the rhythm *(clap twice)*,

The jolly, jolly *(slap knees twice)* rhythm *(clap twice)*,

Ready oh *(slap knees twice)*,

(clap twice — no words)

Let's go *(slap knees twice)*,

(clap twice — no words)

Starting with *(slap knees twice)*

(clap twice — no words)

ZZZZERO *(slap knees twice)*

(clap twice — no words).

Continuing to slap and clap in rhythm, Zero calls out her own number and someone else's number as follows:

Zero, zero *(slap knees twice)*,

Four, four *(clap twice)*.

Without missing a beat, Four responds with his own number, followed by someone else's number. If you call a ghost number or miss a beat, you're out.

35

THE BLAZE

When the fire is ablaze, everyone feels its power. The blaze is hot and exciting. Now is the time to bake pretzels over the campfire or cook corn on the cob underground. Start telling a story or pass around crazy homemade instruments to accompany a singsong.

WHY DOES SMOKE FOLLOW YOU AROUND?

Why is it that wherever you move to escape campfire smoke, on some nights it just keeps following you? On a still night when there's no breeze, try this activity to solve the mystery yourself.

You'll need:

a green stick (like a roasting stick, page 25)

a blazing campfire

1.

Poke the tip of the green stick into the fire until the stick starts smoking.

2.

Lay the smoking stick on the ground 1 m (3 ft.) from the fire in a place where there is nothing burnable that may catch from the hot end of the stick.

3.

Stand well back and watch where the smoke drifts from the stick.

4.

Move the stick to another side of the fire and stand back to watch where the smoke from the stick drifts this time. Continue to move the stick to other sides of the fire and see what happens to the stick's smoke.

5.

Sit down on the ground right behind the smoking end of the stick so it is between you and the fire. What happens to the smoke coming off the stick? Don't rub your eyes — get out of the way!

WHAT'S HAPPENING?

When you stand back from the fire and leave the stick by itself, the smoke from the stick is drawn into the fire. But when you sit beside the stick, the smoke moves toward you and not the fire.

Fire draws in air from all directions, so when you sit beside a campfire on a still night, you block off one of the directions the fire uses to get air. The fire quickly sucks up the air between your body and the flames, leaving a small airless space called a vacuum in front of you. Smoke from the fire moves to fill that vacuum — and gets in your eyes. If you move to another spot, the same thing will happen again. The smoke seems to follow you wherever you go.

To stop smoke from following you, build the campfire next to an object bigger than you, like a large rock or sandbank. Then the smoke will be more attracted to it than to you.

WHAT FLAMES IN A FIRE?

If you look at a campfire, the flames dance above the logs. Believe it or not, the wood itself does not burn. The flames are made from burning gas. When wood is heated, gases in the wood are released, rise above the wood, mix with air and burst into flame. Not all of the heated wood turns into burnable gas. Smoke is made up of gases that do not burn, and the ash you see after a fire is the content of wood that did not turn into gas at all.

You can see this process of making flame by looking at how a match burns. Have an adult light a wooden match and hold the tip upward. The flame dies even though the whole matchstick is there to burn. The heat from the flame rises up and away from the matchstick. The dry wood of the matchstick is not being heated up, so no burnable gases are being released to keep the flame going.

If the match is tipped slightly downward, the flame will catch well. In this case, some of the wood is above the tip and the flame has a chance to warm the wood, releasing gases to feed the flame.

MAKE A REFLECTOR OVEN

With a campfire reflector oven, you can cook just about anything that you can make in a regular oven. The food will have that special smoky campfire taste.

You'll need:

3 aluminum-foil roasting pans

a sharp nail

6 pieces of metal wire cut in 10-cm (4-in.) lengths, or 6 large twist ties with the paper or plastic removed

3 rocks (see page 45, step 5 for rocks to use)

4 flat stones of equal height, pancake size

a small metal grill

1.
One pan will form the back of the oven and the other two will be the sides. Use the nail to punch holes in each of the pans as shown.

2.
Attach the oven back to the sides by threading the wires through the punched holes and twisting the wires together on the outside. Do not tie too tightly — you want to be able to adjust the angle of the sides to get the best heat.

3.
For a small fire, position the oven around three sides of the fire, with the oven's back to the breeze. Use the three rocks to steady the side panels and back. For a large fire, set up the oven beside the hottest side of the fire.

4.
Place four stones of equal height in the middle of the oven to support the grill. A cake rack makes an excellent campfire grill. Metal shelves from old refrigerators or barbecues are the perfect size and are sturdy too.

5.
You can warm food in a pot or foil container placed on the grill or cook right on the grill. Turn to page 42 for some reflector oven recipes.

QUICK AND EASY REFLECTOR

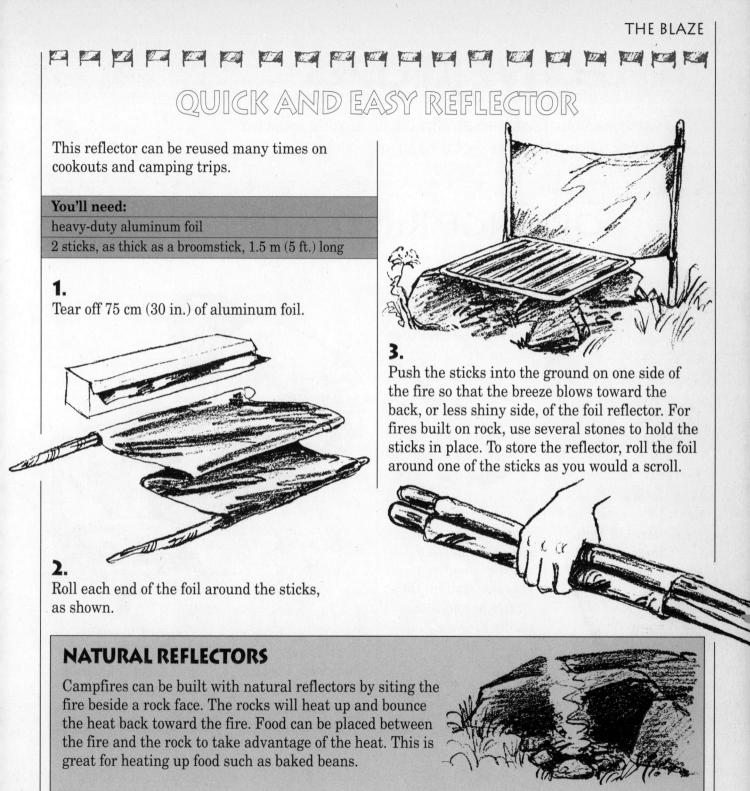

This reflector can be reused many times on cookouts and camping trips.

You'll need:
heavy-duty aluminum foil
2 sticks, as thick as a broomstick, 1.5 m (5 ft.) long

1.

Tear off 75 cm (30 in.) of aluminum foil.

2.

Roll each end of the foil around the sticks, as shown.

3.

Push the sticks into the ground on one side of the fire so that the breeze blows toward the back, or less shiny side, of the foil reflector. For fires built on rock, use several stones to hold the sticks in place. To store the reflector, roll the foil around one of the sticks as you would a scroll.

NATURAL REFLECTORS

Campfires can be built with natural reflectors by siting the fire beside a rock face. The rocks will heat up and bounce the heat back toward the fire. Food can be placed between the fire and the rock to take advantage of the heat. This is great for heating up food such as baked beans.

REFLECTIVE RECIPES

You can cook your favorite campfire foods in your reflector oven, or try baking these reflector oven specialties.

ORANGE RIND MUFFINS

You'll need:
6 oranges
a paring knife
a large spoon
muffin mix
a measuring cup
a bowl or pot
pot holders
a poker

1.
Slice the oranges in half and scoop out and eat or save the fruit. Use a large spoon to scrape out any leftovers.

2.
If the orange half doesn't sit level, cut a sliver of rind from the bottom of it.

3.
Prepare the muffin mix according to the directions on the package. Half fill the orange halves with muffin mixture.

4.
Place the oranges on the grill and watch them bake. Cooking times will vary depending on the heat of the fire, but the muffins should be done in 20 to 25 minutes.

5.
Remove the orange rind muffins from the grill using pot holders and a poker. Allow them to cool for several minutes before eating.
  You can cook your favorite cupcake mix in orange rinds too.

CAMPFIRE COBBLER

You'll need:

500 mL (2c.) berries such as blueberries or raspberries

aluminum foil

50 mL (¼ c.) brown sugar

a bowl or pot

a spoon

50 mL (¼ c.) brown sugar

125 mL (½ c.) flour

125 mL (½ c.) oatmeal

1 mL (¼ tsp.) salt

50 mL (¼ c.) margarine

2 pokers

1.
Place the berries in the center of a piece of foil, about 30 cm (12 in.) long, shiny side facing up.

2.
Pour the honey over the berries.

3.
In the bowl or pot, mix everything else except the margarine together with a spoon.

4.
Pat the mixture over the berries.

5.
Dot the top of the mixture with small pieces of margarine.

6.
Fold the foil around the berries and topping, sealing it all inside.

7.
Place the foil package on the grill for about 30 minutes.

8.
Remove it with two pokers and allow the foil to cool slightly before opening your campfire cobbler to eat. This recipe feeds four to six people.

43

DIG INTO A PIT DINNER

Pit cooking is used at feasting times by Native people all over North America and the South Pacific islands. In Hawaii, a whole pig is cooked in a pit during the famous luau feast. You can cook corn, potatoes, sausages, chicken and other foods a little less enormous than a pig. First you have to get your pit ready. Read all of these instructions before you begin.

You'll need:
an adult helper
two plastic bags
a shovel
flat stones
hardwood for a fire (see pages 12–13)

1.

Collect at least two plastic grocery bags full of fresh green leaves. Starting several days ahead, save vegetable leaves in plastic bags in the fridge. Good greenery to save are carrot tops, the outer leaves of cabbage and lettuce, and corn husks. On the day of the feast, collect seaweed if you are near the ocean and plan to cook clams, crab, lobster or fish. Inland, look for grape, beech, dandelion, fireweed and clover leaves. Handfuls of garden herbs like parsley, tarragon, oregano, chives and thyme add special flavor to the meal.

2.

With an adult, site the pit away from trees, shrubs and buildings. It's a good idea to be near water — a hose will do — because it takes a lot of cold water to cool down the pit at the end. The cooking process is an event in itself, so choose a site where everyone can sit and enjoy the view.

3.

Dig a pit about 1 m (3 ft.) long, 50 cm (20 in.) wide and 50 cm (20 in.) deep. As you dig, pile the sod and dirt to one side of the pit. Keep the piles tidy — the dirt and sod will be used again.

4.

Cut the sod and surface growth back 1 m (3 ft.) all around the pit. Clear the area of burnables such as leaves, twigs and bark. Keep all this in another neat pile away from the fire pit. The day after the feast, you may want to fill in the hole, put the grass on top and make it look like nothing was ever there.

5.

Line the bottom and sides of the pit with medium-sized flat stones. Then, cover the bottom again with smaller stones. Do not use wet stones or layered rocks like shale, which may shatter when they're heated.

6.

About four hours before eating time, start a regular bonfire on the rocks in the pit. Feed it with hardwood, to make a good bed of coals. Keep stoking the fire for about one and a half hours and then let it burn down to hot coals for half an hour. That may take eight hardwood log pieces that are a little thicker than your thigh.

Now you're almost ready for the food. Turn the page to find out how to cook in your pit.

COOKING IN A PIT

Now that you have your pit and fire ready (see page 44), it's time to start cooking.

You'll need:
an adult helper
a rake
a metal grate or grill
at least two pails of water
two bags of leaves or seaweed
kitchen tongs
the food you will cook (see Pit Food for suggestions)
a piece of plywood or a tarpaulin bigger than the pit
a shovel

1.
Two hours before eating time, rake the coals apart. Most of them will drop between the stones in the pit. Pull the bigger coals right out of the pit with the rake and leave them safely on the dirt pile. Work carefully with an adult. Do not touch the rocks, as they are extremely hot.

2.
Ease the metal grate down gently onto the rocks in the pit.

3.
Pour several cupfuls of water on the hot stones.

4.
Drop the leaves from one bag onto the rocks and grate.

5.
Working quickly, use the tongs to place the pieces of meat and the potatoes on the leaves. Drop in another layer of leaves and then lay on the rest of the vegetables. Last of all, place the corn and then the remaining leaves.

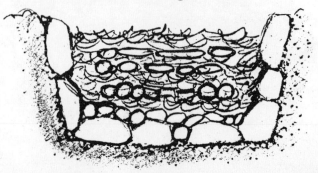

6.

Cover the pit with the plywood or tarpaulin. Shovel dirt to cover the plywood by about 10 cm (4 in.) and seal the edges with dirt. The pit will steam. Keep as much of that steam as possible inside by shoveling dirt over the spots where the steam is escaping. No air should get in or the coals will flame and burn the food.

7.

Once the pit is sealed, leave the dirt and food untouched for about two hours.

8.

Carefully shovel the dirt off the cover and lift the plywood off. Using tongs, lift out the leaves and food, layer by layer, and eat!

SAFETY ALERT

The rocks will remain hot for hours. Before leaving the pit, be sure to pour in pails of water until all the steaming stops.

PIT FOOD

Good vegetables to cook in a pit are:

- corn on the cob (leave the husks on but pull silk tassels out)

- potatoes (leave the skin on but scrub them in water and prick with a fork)

- onions (leave the skin on and prick with a fork)

- green peppers (whole)

Good meats to cook in the fire pit are:

- sausages

- chicken quarters (can be pre-cooked first)

- beef braising ribs

- whole cleaned fish, crab, lobster, clams in the shells (Eat only clams that open with cooking.)

JAZZING UP A SING-ALONG

Everyone loves singing around a campfire. You can add to the fun by making some simple rhythm instruments. Then turn to the song section on page 94 and choose some of your favorites to sing.

SHAKERS

You'll need:

an iced tea can, half full with crystals, or an empty, clean coffee can and lid

rice, dried peas or small pebbles

1.
The half-full iced tea can makes a great shaker, or you can make one by half filling the coffee can with rice, peas, pebbles or a mixture of these. Be sure the lids are on tight.

2.
Hold the container sideways in one hand and shake it quickly so the contents hit one end and slide back to hit the other. Do this with each beat of the music. When you get the hang of it, try shaking on the half beat or slowly, on every second or third beat.

TAMBOURINE

You'll need:

a small handful of dried peas or small pebbles

2 aluminum-foil pie plates

masking tape

1.
Pour the peas or pebbles into one of the pie plates.

2.
Cover it with the other plate.

3.
Tape around the outside where the pie plates meet, sealing the seam well.

4.
Shake the tambourine with one hand to make a dry, jingling sound. With the other hand, tap the outside of the plates to the rhythm of the music. Make different tones by using your fingertips, knuckles, wrist or your palm.

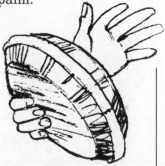

48

SPOONS

DRUMS

SPOONS

You'll need:

a pair of small wooden or metal spoons with narrow handles

1.
With one hand, hold the spoons by their handles so the bowls are back to back. Hold the handles loosely between your thumb and middle finger. Slip the tip of your index finger between the handles.

2.
Shake your hand so the backs of the spoons clack together. Adjust your grip until you can control the beat and move your hand around too.

3.
Practice striking the side of your hand on your thigh as you continue to clack the spoons together. Next, try holding your free hand above your leg so the spoons hit your hand too.

DRUMS

You'll need:

empty containers such as cardboard ice cream tubs, plastic waste baskets, clay flowerpots

fat, rounded knitting needles, chopsticks or tree sticks

tape or string

metal nuts, brush bristles, buttons or beads

1.
Knitting needles, chopsticks and sticks can be used for drumsticks as they are. Or, you can get different effects by taping or tying metal nuts, buttons or brush bristles to the sticks.

2.
Turn the containers upside down on a flat surface.

3.
Hold one drumstick in each hand and hit the drum containers to the beat of the song. Experiment with adding new beats and new sounds. A good drummer finds the heartbeat of a song.

WILD SOUND

There are lots of wild sounds you can add to a campfire singsong. Bang two sticks together, strike a hollow log, run a stick along the side of a bristling pine cone, swirl pebbles around in a cup. Use your imagination and keep that beat!

DOLL-FACE SINGING

For some wild laughter at your campfire, make a headless doll and put on a show.

You'll need:
2 pairs of old pantyhose
cotton stuffing
a needle
thread
nail polish or white glue
scissors
2 pieces of fabric 40 cm x 40 cm (16 in. x 16 in.)
straight pins
a piece of elastic 50 cm (20 in.) long
a safety pin
washable markers

1.

The pantyhose form the arms and legs of the doll. Push the cotton stuffing into the feet and legs of the pantyhose, filling one pair to measure 25 cm (10 in.) long and the other pair to measure 20 cm (8 in.) long.

2.

Sew back and forth above the stuffing of each pair to close them up. Apply a line of nail polish or white glue above the stitching to prevent the pantyhose from running. Allow it to dry and then cut off the extra pantyhose 2.5 cm (1 in.) above the polish or glue.

3.

Lay one square of material on a table with the pattern side up. Place an arm on each side of the square and pin them about halfway down the square. Sew the arms in place.

4.

Keeping the arms on the inside, place the second square of fabric over the first with the pattern side down. Pin the sides together and sew down 2 cm ($^3/_4$ in.) from the edge, through all the thicknesses.

5.

Turn the fabric right side out. Pin up 2 cm (³/₄ in.) from the bottom, pinning the legs in place, as shown. Sew the legs in place and remove the pins, then sew around the bottom edge, stitching through all thicknesses.

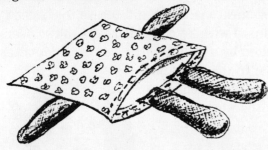

6.

Fold 2.5 cm (1 in.) of fabric from the top edge to the inside and pin it in place. Sew around the top, leaving a gap of 2 cm (³/₄ in.) at one side seam.

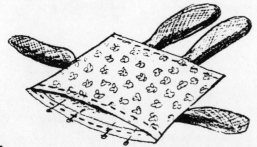

7.

Measure the elastic to fit around your head plus 5 cm (2 in.). Attach a safety pin to one end of the elastic and slip it through the gap. Pin the loose end to one side of the gap in the seam. Work the safety pin around the inside and out the gap again.

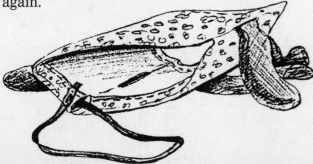

8.

Adjust the tightness of the elastic to fit loosely around your head. Tie the two ends of the elastic in a knot.

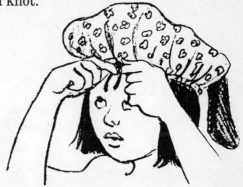

9.

Draw eyes on your chin with the washable marker, then pull the doll body over your face and head. Lie flat on a table or rock, hanging your head over the edge. Face your audience and sing your favorite campfire song. Try to get everyone to sing along — if they can stop laughing.

FAMILY STORIES

These story starters will get you going on an evening of revealing storytelling.

EVERY SCAR TELLS A TALE

How did Uncle Stephen get the stitches on his chin? Did he trip while chasing a girl in the schoolyard when he was a boy? You'll never know until you play this game.

Take turns around the campfire circle describing how you got the most unusual scar on your body. Most people will have chicken pox marks or surgical stitches, but has anyone the tell-tale marks of a mean fish? It's okay to tell the tale, but you don't have to reveal the scar itself.

I'M NOT EATING THAT!

Have you ever been served super-sour rhubarb pie or burnt macaroni and cheese that's been disguised with ketchup? Perhaps you've been revolted by a meal prepared at camp, on a school trip or in the cafeteria? Try to outdo each other with the worst meal ever — just make sure everyone's finished eating first.

EMBARRASS THE ADULTS

Asking the adults around the campfire some questions about their youth can lead to some interesting, and surprising, stories. Ask them about their first kiss. Did they ever get in trouble at school? How did your parents or grandparents meet? Why not ask all the adults to tell about their most embarrassing moment.

FAMILY TWENTY QUESTIONS

If your campfire gathering consists of only family, you can personalize this game to suit the group. Play with the same rules as Twenty Questions on page 54. The objects are then connected with a family member. For example, Susan's coin collection would be a mineral, Grandma's piano is both vegetable and mineral, Uncle Ed's big toe would be animal, Sam's red bicycle is mineral and the family dog's drool is definitely animal.

MORE CAMPFIRE GAMES

Sharpen your wits and have fun too with these brain-teasing campfire games.

TWENTY QUESTIONS

Also known as Animal, Vegetable or Mineral, this is a word-guessing game played by at least two people or two teams. One person can be designated as the judge to referee any disputes.

Animal means any living thing — from a blue whale to the tiniest flea.

Vegetable refers to all plant life and things made from it, such as poison ivy and wooden stools.

Mineral includes all non-living things such as fossils or plastic toys.

One person thinks of an object. The group then asks up to 20 questions to identify the object, usually asking first if it is an animal, vegetable or mineral. The answers can be only yes or no. The person or team that guesses the object chooses the next one. If no one guesses, the person takes another turn.

IN THE MANNER OF THE WORD

This is an acting game similar to charades, where players must show the answer by their actions, not their words.

Divide into two teams. Team 1 thinks of an adverb that ends in "-ly," such as "slowly." One player on Team 2 is told the adverb. She must get her team to guess the adverb by acting out the word.

For example, Team 2 asks its actor to add a piece of wood to the fire "in the manner of the word." The actor adds a piece of wood to the fire "slowly." The team calls out possible adverbs — "carefully," "quietly," "timidly," etc. The actor encourages her team by shaking her head for no or nodding to indicate that her team is getting close. If the right word is not called, the team chooses another action for the actor to mime and tries to guess another adverb. If the right word is said, Team 1 takes a turn.

THE DOUBLE LETTER GAME

Here's a brain-teasing word game that will boggle your mind. Think of a word that has the same two letters, side by side, such as "trees." Then think of a word that is connected to it but does not have a double letter, such as "leaves." Start the game by saying, "I love trees, but I hate leaves." If no one catches on to the pattern, give another example, such as "I love boots, but I hate shoes." As people get the idea that the first word always has a double letter and the second doesn't, they join in with their own examples. Keep thinking of examples until everyone around the fire has figured it out. Can you think of any that relate to the campfire? What about "I love wood, but I hate smoke"?

HOT COALS

When the blaze settles down to hot coals, it's the best time for cooking on the campfire. Without flame, your food will brown nicely instead of burning right away. If you've been stoking the fire with sweet-smelling hardwoods such as maple, hickory, apple or cherry, the food will take on a delicious smoky flavor too.

Read on and find out how to roast a spider dog, toast a bannock twist, grill a cheese sandwich or bake a potato. While the food is cooking, you can watch the rising Moon or do some stargazing.

COOKING IN THE COALS

Cooking over the coals is fun, and the food tastes delicious. If you have a bed of coals with some logs on top still giving off flame, use your poker to separate the logs. Then the flame will quiet down and the logs will start to glow with the rest of the coals.

ROAST A HOT DOG

Spear a wiener at one end with a roasting stick (see page 25) so that the stick runs partway up the length of the wiener. Be sure the meat is well attached so that it doesn't fall into the coals!

Hold the stick above the coals. Find a spot where your hands and body are comfortably away from the heat, but the wiener is close enough to cook. Turn the stick slowly until the wiener is brown on all sides. Do not let it burn — it doesn't take long for a wiener to warm through. When it is cooked to your liking, slip it off the stick into a bun. Dress it up with ketchup, relish and mustard. Let it cool a little before taking your first bite.

SPIDER DOG

If you like eating your hot dog without a bun, try making a spider dog. Poke your roasting stick in one end of a wiener partway up its length. With a knife, carefully make two cuts in the free end of the wiener. Roast it until the cut pieces sizzle and curl back. Remove the wiener from the heat and let it cool a minute. Now, pull the wiener off the stick and put it back on the other way. Cut two slices into the end now pointing away from the stick. Roast until those cut pieces brown and curl. Let the wiener cool a minute on the stick. Eat your spider right off the stick, wiggly legs and all!

BANNOCK DOG

Here's a way to make dough for a bun and cook it right on the wiener over the campfire. Bannock, or wilderness bread, puffs up a little and makes a yummy, chewy bun. This recipe will make four bannock hot dogs.

You'll need:

250 mL (1 c.) flour

a pinch of salt

10 mL (2 tsp.) baking powder

a bowl

5 mL (1 tsp.) margarine

125 mL (½ c.) milk or water

a fork

a little extra flour

4 wieners

4 roasting sticks

1.
Combine the flour, salt and baking powder in the bowl.

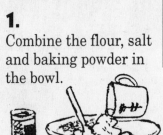

2.
Add the margarine and pinch all the ingredients together between your finger tips. Wipe off your hands on a clean cloth.

3.
Add the milk or water slowly as you mix everything with a fork. Stir until a stiff dough is formed.

4.
With floured fingers, mix the dough a little more until it is smooth. Don't handle it too much or it will get tough.

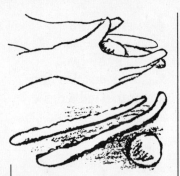

5.
Divide the dough into four balls. Roll the balls between your palms to create long worms of dough.

6.
Spear each uncooked wiener onto a roasting stick so the stick runs up the length of the wiener. Twist the dough along each wiener.

7.
Roast your hot dog bannock twist as you would a regular hot dog, but a little farther away from the coals. Take your time: it takes about 8 minutes for the dough to puff into a tasty, ready-to-eat bun-dog combo. Let it cool a little before you bite into it.

59

GRILLED CHEESE SANDWICH

You can cook that old favorite, the grilled cheese sandwich, over a campfire.

You'll need:

a green stick grill (see page 25)

two slices of bread

a slice of cheese

1.
Lay one slice of bread on the green stick grill and brown the bottom side over the coals. Put it aside and toast the second piece of bread on one side.

2.
Place the cheese between the two toasted sides, leaving the untoasted sides facing out.

3.
Lay the whole sandwich back on the green stick grill, and lightly toast one uncooked side and then the other.

4.
Leave it a minute to cool, dip in ketchup and eat.

CAMPFIRE PIZZA

These mini-pizzas are great cooked over the campfire.

You'll need:

a green stick grill (see page 25)

half an English muffin

25 mL (2 tbsp.) ketchup or tomato sauce

slices of your favorite toppings such as pepperoni, mushrooms, onion and green pepper

25 mL (2 tbsp.) grated cheese

1.
Lay the muffin on a green stick grill and toast the top side to a golden brown.

2.
Turn the muffin over. On the toasted side, spread ketchup, your favorite toppings and finally the cheese.

3.
Toast the bottom side slowly, well above the coals so it won't burn. Let the toppings heat through until the cheese starts to melt.

4.
Let the pizza cool a little before eating it.

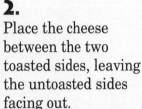

FOIL POTATOES

Baked potatoes are easy to cook in the coals. Afterward, you can dress them up with terrific toppings.

You'll need:
scrubbed, unpeeled potatoes
a fork, knife and spoon
aluminum foil
a poker (see page 20)
toppings such as sour cream, butter, grated cheese and bacon bits

1.
Prick each potato with the fork a few times.

2.
Wrap each potato well with aluminum foil, shiny side in.

3.
Place the potatoes at the edge of the coals. After half an hour, flip the potatoes over with your poker and then leave them for another half hour.

4.
After an hour, ask an adult to prick one potato with a fork. If the fork goes in easily, the potato is cooked and you can take it out of the coals with the fork. If the fork hits a hard potato, let it cook longer.

CORN ON THE COB

Corn cooks well in the coals too. Peel back the green husk leaves of the corn cob enough to pull out the silk tassels. Close up the leaves again and soak the whole cob in water. Once the leaves are good and wet, place the cob at the edge of the coals. After 15 minutes, roll the corn out of the coals with your fire poker and allow it to cool for several minutes. Prick the kernels with a fork to be sure they are soft enough to eat. If the kernels need more cooking, roll the cob back into the coals.

5.
Allow the potatoes to cool for several minutes before unwrapping the foil. Potatoes stay hot for a long time, so be careful.

6.
Slit each potato open with a knife and add your favorite toppings. Eat it like a sandwich or with a knife and fork. Enjoy!

SUMMER STARGAZING

On a clear, moonless night, away from city lights, the stars look brighter and some even shine in color — red, blue and yellow. You can identify some stars and groups of stars, called constellations, with the summer star map on the next page.

HOW TO USE A STAR MAP

Find a comfortable place to sit or lie where the whole sky is in view. Look north and hold the star map in front of you with the word "North" at the bottom of the map. Or, look south and hold the star map with the word "South" at the bottom. You may find that reading the words on your star map is difficult at night, even with a flashlight. Human eyes have trouble focusing when they move from a lit page to dark sky and back again. Tie a red bandanna around the end of your flashlight, to cast a glow that makes it easier for your eyes to switch between map and sky. Use your red light and star map to find star and constellation names.

NIGHTWATCH

Have you noticed that night falls earlier on a campfire evening in August than in June? June 21 is the longest day and shortest night of a northern year. On that day, the Sun has traveled as far north as it ever does. After June 21, until December 21, the Sun moves farther and farther south. On December 21, the shortest day and longest night of our year, the Sun stops traveling south and turns north again. So, the Sun sets and night falls earlier in August than in June.

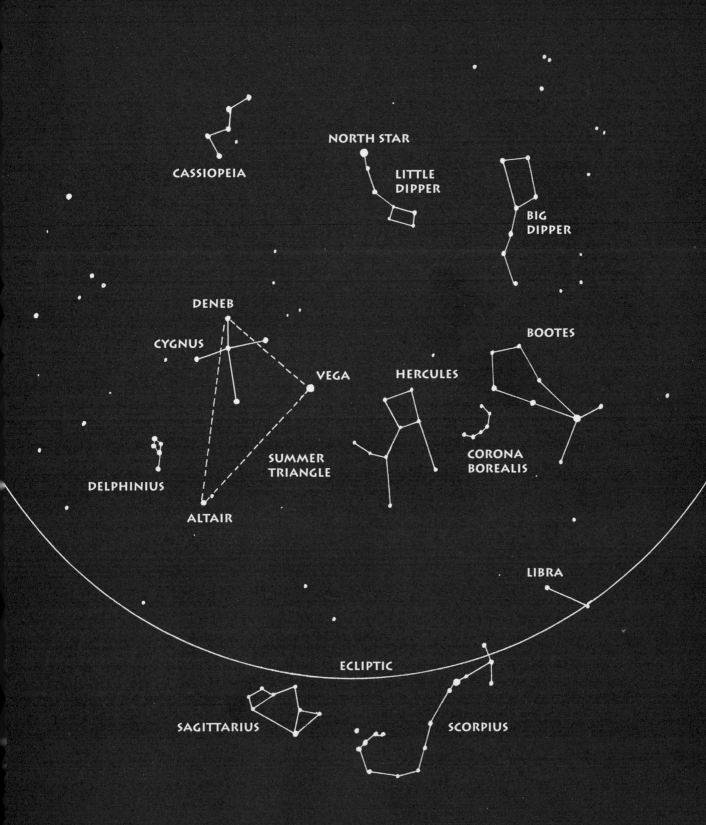

CASSIOPEIA

NORTH STAR

LITTLE
DIPPER

BIG
DIPPER

DENEB

CYGNUS

BOOTES

VEGA

HERCULES

DELPHINIUS

SUMMER
TRIANGLE

CORONA
BOREALIS

ALTAIR

LIBRA

ECLIPTIC

SAGITTARIUS

SCORPIUS

STAR SEARCH

The Milky Way, the Big Dipper, the Summer Triangle and Hercules are the star attractions of the summer night sky. Once you have located them, use the star map on page 63 to find other interesting constellations and heavenly sights.

THE MILKY WAY

Look for a wide band of stars that runs north to south across the sky. Ancient people thought these stars blurred together like a river of milk. The Milky Way is part of our own huge galaxy, and the Sun is a minor star between the center and one edge of the galaxy.

At the southern base of the Milky Way, Sagittarius looks like a teapot. To the ancient Greeks, this constellation was a centaur, half man, half horse. Scorpius, the Scorpion, looks like a huge fishhook on the southern horizon. Ancient Chinese people called it a dragon. The red supergiant star, Antares, is its heart. Antares is 700 times larger than our Sun.

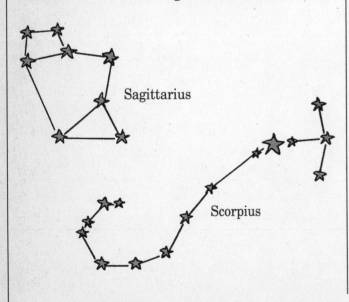

Sagittarius

Scorpius

THE BIG DIPPER AND CASSIOPEIA

This constellation in the north looks like a long-handled pot. Many ancient peoples saw a bear in the stars around and including the Big Dipper. The bowl of the Dipper is the bear's body and the handle is its tail. No bears alive today have long tails.

Find the North Star by following where water would pour from the bowl of the Dipper. If you watch the North Star throughout the night, all other stars seem to circle around it. This is because Earth turns one full circle every day under the North Star.

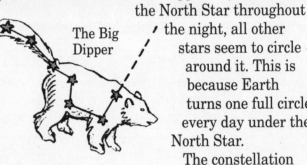

The Big Dipper

The constellation Cassiopeia, or the wobbly W at the north end of the Milky Way, sits on the other side of the North Star from the Big Dipper. Cassiopeia was a legendary queen who boasted that her daughter was more beautiful than any sea nymph. This angered the sea god, who sent a monster to devour the girl. At the last moment, the hero Perseus was able to save her. Now all the characters in the story have a place in the stars and Queen Cassiopeia still watches over her family.

Cassiopeia

THE SUMMER TRIANGLE

The Summer Triangle is made up of three of the brightest stars in the night sky — Vega, Altair and Deneb. Almost directly overhead is Vega, a brilliant, blue-white star. To Vega's east in the Milky Way is Deneb. Deneb is a distant, blue-white supergiant star, 60 000 times more powerful than our Sun. South of Deneb and also in the Milky Way is yellow Altair, the closest star to Earth in the Triangle.

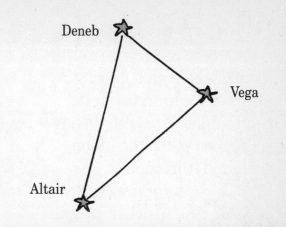

HERCULES, CORONA BOREALIS AND BOOTES

West of Vega is the constellation Hercules. Hercules was a Greek hero who took on 12 great challenges, called labors, to rid the world of deadly monsters. Hercules is usually seen carrying a lion-skin shield and a heavy club. In the black, starless space beside Hercules, you will see a fuzzy ball of light at the edge of your vision. This is a cluster of thousands of stars, best seen when you are not looking directly at it!

West of Hercules is the small, dazzling crown of stars called Corona Borealis. Farther west is a group of stars that looks like a kite. The orange giant star, Arcturus, is at its base. The ancient Greeks called this constellation Bootes, the Herdsman.

FINDING THE PLANETS

The curved line on the star map on page 63 is called the ecliptic. The Sun, planets, Moon and other objects in our solar system take this path as they move across the sky. Look for Venus, Mars, Jupiter, Saturn and tiny Mercury at different times along the ecliptic.

MOONWATCH

The Moon has been a guest at campfires since humans first learned to make fire. People have always looked up at the Moon and included it in their campfire stories. Ancient people thought the Moon was a hole in the sky, possibly leading to heaven. Later Europeans gazed at the Moon's features and saw a man up there. The Chinese saw a gentle rabbit. For some, the Moon's face looked cold and suggested madness. The words "loony," "lunatic" and "loon" come from old Latin and French words for Moon — "lune." Storytellers linked the Moon with evil and invented such creatures as werewolves, ghouls and vampires.

THE MOON AND WILDLIFE

When the Moon is full, the night can be so bright that trees and rocks cast shadows. On these bright nights, listen for the chirps and songs of daytime birds like American Robins, Wood Thrushes, White-throated Sparrows, Ovenbirds and Red-winged Blackbirds.

Some people believe that nightloving creatures are more active during a full Moon too, but scientists have discovered that this is not true. Loons call back and forth to their family members at night whether the Moon is out or not. As far as scientists know, wolves howl not to the Moon, but to each other.

THE CHANGING MOON

The Moon moves around Earth every $29\frac{1}{2}$ days. Together, Earth and the Moon circle the Sun. The Sun shines on half the Moon, but we see only the lighted part that faces us. Once every $29\frac{1}{2}$ days we see a full Moon, when the entire lighted part of the Moon faces Earth. Once every Moon cycle we also see no Moon, or new Moon, when the entire lighted part of the Moon is facing away from Earth. Native Americans measured time and distance by Moon cycles. They talked of distant places as being several Moons away, meaning several complete Moon cycles away.

MOON CYCLE

Day 1
new Moon

Day 3
crescent Moon

Day 7
first quarter Moon

Day 10
near-full Moon

Day 14
full Moon

Day 20
past-full Moon

Day 22
last quarter Moon

Day 28
crescent Moon

FACES OF THE MOON

If you look at the Moon through binoculars you can see valleys, or craters, and mountains. Look along the line where sunlight and darkness meet on the face of the Moon. This line is called the terminator. The craters and mountains stand out most clearly near the terminator because the shadows are strongest there.

THE MAN IN THE MOON

There are two times in the Moon cycle to spot a face on the Moon, usually called the man in the Moon. The first time is Day 10, between the first quarter and the full Moon. (See page 67 for Moon cycles.) At this time, the man in the Moon looks jolly. The second time is when the Moon is full. This man in the Moon has a more serious face.

THE JOLLY FACE IN THE MOON

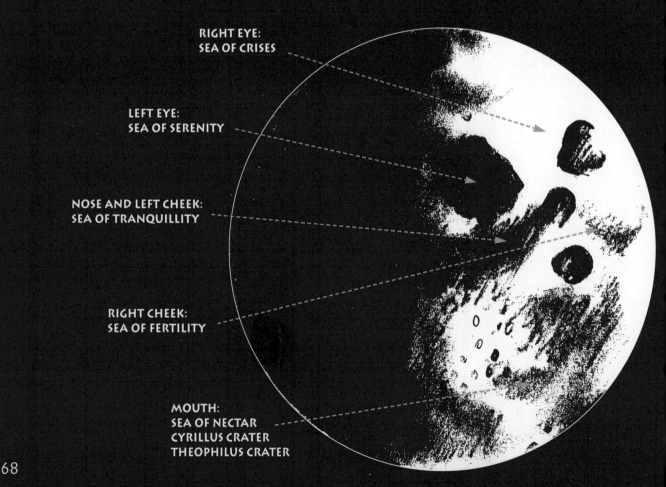

RIGHT EYE:
SEA OF CRISES

LEFT EYE:
SEA OF SERENITY

NOSE AND LEFT CHEEK:
SEA OF TRANQUILLITY

RIGHT CHEEK:
SEA OF FERTILITY

MOUTH:
SEA OF NECTAR
CYRILLUS CRATER
THEOPHILUS CRATER

The eyes, nose and mouth on the faces are made up of huge dark grey areas called seas. Early Moon watchers thought these dark areas were bodies of water. We now know they are dry plains covered with dark lava rock. As you look at the man in the Moon with your binoculars, see if you can find the seas and some of the craters.

THE SERIOUS FACE IN THE MOON

LEFT EYE:
SEA OF RAINS (WHERE "LUNA 2" LANDED, THE FIRST ROCKET TO REACH THE MOON IN 1959) COPERNICUS CRATER

RIGHT EYE:
SEA OF TRANQUILLITY (WHERE "APOLLO 11" LANDED IN 1969 AND THE FIRST MOON WALK TOOK PLACE)

NOSE:
CENTRAL BAY

MOUTH:
SEA OF CLOUDS CLAVIUS CRATER TYCHO CRATER

MOTHS AND THE CAMPFIRE

Wildlife is usually afraid of fire. Start a campfire and raccoons, porcupines, squirrels, spiders, crickets and other animals will all move away. But moths seem unafraid of fire. They fly round and round a fire and into the smoke. Some moths will even fly right into the flame. Read on to find out why.

MOONBEAMS AND MOTHS

Scientists believe that moths find their way in the dark by tracking moonbeams. Just as boaters keep on course by steering for a distant landmark, night-flying moths navigate by making sure the moonlight falls on their wings from one direction only. Lights and campfires confuse them. If the light cast from a campfire is quite blue, like moonlight, moths are attracted to it. They fly around and around a strong, blue flame, unable to find their bearings. When the poor moth has become exhausted and cannot fly any more, it falls into the fire and sizzles up.

NIGHT-FLYING MOTHS

Some moths fly by day, but most are night fliers. Here are some to look for by the campfire. If one gets too close, you can help it by brushing it gently away from the fire.

BANDED WOOLLYBEAR

A small, pale brown moth with black spots. The Woollybear is best known in its caterpillar stage as it crosses lawns and roads to find a winter home.

UNDERWING MOTH

This moth has dull gray upper wings, but beautiful underwings that flash with black and pink or orange patterns when it flies.

TIGER MOTH

This moth's upper wings have a pretty pale yellow and black pattern and its underwings are a bold orange color with black spots. The Tiger Moth's bright colors warn its enemies that it is poisonous to eat.

GIANT SILKWORM MOTHS

The pale green Luna Moth and the Polyphemus Moth with blue and yellow eye-spots on its wings are both so big, they can be confused with bats.

NIGHT SMELLERS

The delicate antennae at the tip of a moth's body are really its nose. Many moths drink nectar from flowers. They find the flowers by smelling the perfume with their antennae. Male moths also use their antennae to find a mate. The female moths give off a scent that the male detects with his antennae and follows to find the female.

STILL MORE GAMES

Some people think that the Moon makes people do funny things. See if you agree, after playing these loony games.

NO LAUGHING

How long can you keep a straight face? Choose someone to go first. Without making a sound, he walks around the circle making the craziest face possible. Keep going until everyone has laughed or at least smiled. The last person to give in and laugh goes next.

You can also try having everyone laugh *except* the person who is walking around the circle. It's hard to keep a straight face while everyone else is cackling and howling.

BUNNY EARS

One person in the circle begins by waving her hands (bunny ears) above her ears. The person on her left waves only his right hand and the person on her right waves his left hand. Then the main bunny pretends to throw her ears to someone on the other side of the circle. That person starts to wave his ears and the people on each side wave one ear. You're out if you get mixed up and don't wave the correct ear or ears.

HULA HOOP PASS

If you don't have a hula hoop, it's worth getting one to see your friends and family tie themselves in knots over this game.

Everyone stands in a circle. One person slips a hula hoop over his arm and then everyone joins hands. Now pass the hula hoop all the way around the circle without ever letting go of anyone's hands. This is really fun when you have a mix of kids and adults in your circle.

FRIENDLY KNOTS

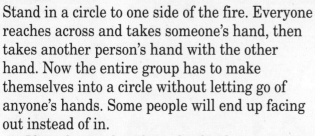

Stand in a circle to one side of the fire. Everyone reaches across and takes someone's hand, then takes another person's hand with the other hand. Now the entire group has to make themselves into a circle without letting go of anyone's hands. Some people will end up facing out instead of in.

If you have a lot of people, divide into two or three smaller groups and see who can untangle themselves the fastest.

FORTUNATELY, UNFORTUNATELY

Fill a bag with lots of everyday things that are not breakable or sharp. You could put in a toilet plunger, a teddy bear, a fly swatter, a toilet-paper roll, bird feathers and a fossil. Sit around the campfire and use the items from the bag to create a wacky story. Decide who is going to start and begin with something like this:

"Jennifer was ready to drive Aunt Jane's new van. (Draw an object from the bag.) Fortunately, she had her trusty plunger." (Pass the plunger to the next person, who continues the story.)

"She tied the plunger to the side-view mirror and climbed in the car. (Reach into the bag and draw out the next prop.) Unfortunately, there was a bear in the trunk." (Pass the teddy bear to the next person, who continues the story.) Alternate between "Fortunately" and "Unfortunately" until the bag is empty. The person with the last object ends the story with a dramatic event.

73

THE LAST EMBERS

When the coals turn to embers, the heat and glow of the campfire fade. The small pieces left in the fire are mostly covered in white ash with a few spots still glowing. Make your dessert now, before the heat is all gone. Listen to the night sounds beyond the fire — hoots, snufflings, snorts and grunts. You may see bats flying without hearing them. The time is perfect for ghost stories as people huddle closer together.

DESSERT!

Before the coals turn completely to ash, make your dessert. A well-roasted marshmallow is always yummy. Or you can try something fancier like smores or banana boats.

ROASTING A MARSHMALLOW

All you need to roast a marshmallow is a good roasting stick (see page 25) and a regular-sized marshmallow (not mini-sized). There are two ways to cook a marshmallow:

VERSION 1

Hold the marshmallow on its stick above the coals and slowly turn it to brown the outside evenly and to cook the inside. After letting it cool, eat the marshmallow right off the stick.

VERSION 2

Put the marshmallow into the flame. As soon as it has burned black, take it out of the fire and let it cool. If the marshmallow catches fire, *gently* blow out the flame and let it cool. Pull off the black shell and eat the warm and creamy insides only.

SMORES

You'll need:
regular-sized marshmallows
a bar of chocolate
graham crackers

1. Roast your marshmallow to a golden brown.

2. Make a gooey sandwich by placing the marshmallow and a piece of chocolate between two graham crackers.

3. Lick your fingers and say, "I want s'more smores — please!"

BANANA BOATS

ROASTED APPLE

You'll need:

bananas
a knife
mini-marshmallows or cut-up regular-sized marshmallows
chocolate chips
aluminum foil
a poker (see page 20)
a spoon

1.
Peel open one side of a banana. Leave the peeled skin dangling from the fruit.

2.
Cut out a length of banana where the skin is open. Eat the slice.

3.
Fill the cut with mini-marshmallows and chocolate chips.

4.
Cover the filling with the piece of banana skin.

5.
Wrap the whole banana in aluminum foil, shiny side facing in.

6.
Lay the banana boat on the dying coals for 15 minutes.

7.
Pull the banana boat from the fire with a poker. When it has cooled, peel open the skin again and eat the yummy insides with a spoon.

You'll need:

a knife
an apple
brown sugar
fillings such as raisins, mini-marshmallows or chocolate chips
cinnamon
aluminum foil
a poker

1.
Cut a circle around the core of the apple at the top and take out as much of the core as you can. Save the cap with the twig attached.

2.
Fill the apple with brown sugar and fillings, then sprinkle with a little cinnamon. Replace the cap.

3.
Wrap the apple in aluminum foil, shiny side in, and place it in the dying coals for about 15 minutes.

4.
Pull the apple out of the fire with a poker. When the foil has cooled, open it up and bite into your roasted apple.

BATWATCH

When dusk is falling and the light is spooky, watch for bats swooping about beyond the campfire, feasting on mosquitoes, flies and moths.

Most North American bats are insect eaters. They migrate south for the winter to find food and return each summer to northern country. Bats use their ears for nighttime hunting. In flight, the bat makes a high pitched noise that bounces or echoes off everything in its path, including people, trees and bugs. Fortunately, bats know which objects are food and zero in on the insect, using their mouths and wings to catch it. This method of finding prey is called echolocation.

Bats have an unusual way of sleeping too. They sleep upside down in large groups called colonies. They like buildings with high ceilings — like churches and barns. If you have a hollow tree with woodpecker holes or unused bird houses in shady spots, bats might move in to roost.

BATTY HIDE-AND-SEEK

The object of this game is to hide and not be found but also to confuse the seekers by making the noise of a nocturnal, or night, animal.

Set the boundaries of this game so you don't lose anyone in the dark and stay well away from the waterfront. Choose a home base — why not the campfire? Decide who are hiders and who are seekers. You'll need three hiders for each seeker. Each hider needs a small stick to hide with.

Give the hiders at least a minute to get hidden properly. Find a spot to hide where you blend in with the surroundings and snuggle down. Think of a night noise to repeat quietly — an owl's whoo, the soft call of the whippoorwill, or listen to the natural noises around you and try imitating one.

When a seeker finds a hider, the hider hands over the stick. The hider can return to home base or hide again and make night noises to confuse the seekers. When the seekers have as many sticks as there are hiders, they call "Awlly, in come." Meet back at home base before you switch around roles to play again.

ECOWATCH

Naturalists call bats sensitive bioindicators. They are a sign of a thriving, healthy natural world, and their absence is a warning of environmental trouble. If you see bats on your property, it means the air and water are healthy.

79

NIGHT HOWLS

Night sounds are often frightening. Even ordinary sounds like lapping waves or rustling leaves can be scary if you are not expecting them. But no night sound compares to the wild howl of a wolf. Wolves howl for different reasons — to stake out their territory or to locate other members of the pack. Sometimes, they howl to signal the beginning or end of a hunt. Wolves may also howl just for fun.

SAFETY ALERT

Healthy wild animals, including wolves, are afraid of people. If any wild animal approaches you, get out of its way. A friendly wild animal may be sick or injured and could be dangerous.

HOW TO ORGANIZE A WOLF HOWL

On a late summer night in the wilderness, you can sometimes trick wolves into howling. All you have to do is howl, and if the young or adults are listening, they may respond.

To start a wolf howl, get several friends together. Stand facing in the direction of the deepest wilderness. One person throws back her head and howls from deep in the throat. The sound should be a loud, long howl and not a yell. If it echoes back from distant hills, that's good — the howl is traveling far.

Then, keep quiet and listen for at least 30 seconds. If there is no answer, try again. If there is still no answer on the third try, everyone else can add howls to make an overlapping chorus. Someone can even add the yips of young. After about 30 seconds, everyone should stop and listen. If there is no response, try again. If there is still no answer after three group howls, wait for another night. The wolves are either not there or do not feel like answering. If wolves do respond, rest up your throats. They will not respond again until about half an hour later. But they are out there, waiting and listening!

OTHER NIGHT CRIES

chirping
cricket

buzzing, whining
mosquito

peeping
spring frog

long, melodic trilling
tree frog or toad

hooting
owl

the Barred Owl's hoots make
the rhythm

> "who cooks for you . . .
> who cooks for you all"

the Horned Owl's hoots
make the rhythm

> "who hoohoo who . . .
> who who"

barking (almost like coughing)
fox

yipping
coyote

blood-curdling screaming
raccoons fighting

wailing
loon calling for mate or young

quavering yodel or wild laughing
loon calling with alarm

repeated, short buzzing
nighthawk

81

GHOST STORIES

As the fire fades, night darkens the edges of the campfire circle and everyone draws closer. Firelight flickers eerily on people's hands and faces, sounds from beyond the circle seem loud and unfamiliar. The mood is right for a ghost story.

To be a good ghost storyteller, keep your voice low, speak slowly and use thoughtful pauses now and then. If you can work it into the story, hint that the events happened to you or someone you know. Hold a flashlight turned on under your chin to add a spooky effect. Try the stories on the next pages.

THE HITCHHIKER

We were driving along past the cemetery on a dark night not long ago. The rain was coming down in sheets. Suddenly I called out "Stop" to Mom. In our headlights I could see a boy on the side of the road. He was wearing only a T-shirt and shorts.

We stopped and he got into the back seat. He didn't talk much, but I remember he said his name was Jack. I soon noticed he was shivering and wet, so I offered him my sweatshirt.

He asked us to stop at the end of a driveway and he jumped out. When he got to the front door of his house, we drove off. It wasn't until later that I remembered he still had on my sweatshirt.

The next day, we had to drive down the same road to town, so Mom stopped at the house. We walked up to the door and knocked. An old man and woman answered and Mom told about offering Jack a ride in the rain and about the sweatshirt.

The old man said there had to be some mistake. Their son had been called Jack, but he died 25 years ago the night before. He was buried in the local cemetery.

When we got to town Mom was doing the shopping, so I walked to the cemetery and looked for his grave.

When I found Jack's headstone, lying on the ground in front of it was my sweatshirt, covered in leaves and soil.

83

A JUMP STORY

This traditional ghost story is known as a "jump" story. The line "Where is my golden arm?" is said more scarily each time it is repeated. The last line of the story is yelled out loudly. The effect is to make everyone "jump" with fright.

THE GOLDEN ARM

A man and a woman, who used to live near here, were in a car accident. The woman lost her arm. The husband felt so guilty he bought his wife a golden arm.

Soon the man began to think of all the things he could buy with the gold in the arm and plotted to kill his wife. But, strangely enough, she died of natural causes before he could carry out his plan. He stole her golden arm from the coffin before she was buried.

The first night after her funeral, he was lying in bed when he thought he heard a voice moaning in the wind outside. "Where is my golden arm?"

He told himself he must be hearing things and soon fell asleep.

The next night, about midnight, he heard a moaning just outside the front door. "Where is my golden arm?"

It took a little longer before he fell asleep.

The third night, the man locked the front door and pushed a chair under the doorknob. He fell asleep, but around midnight he heard a moaning that seemed to come from right outside his bedroom door. This time he thought it was

84

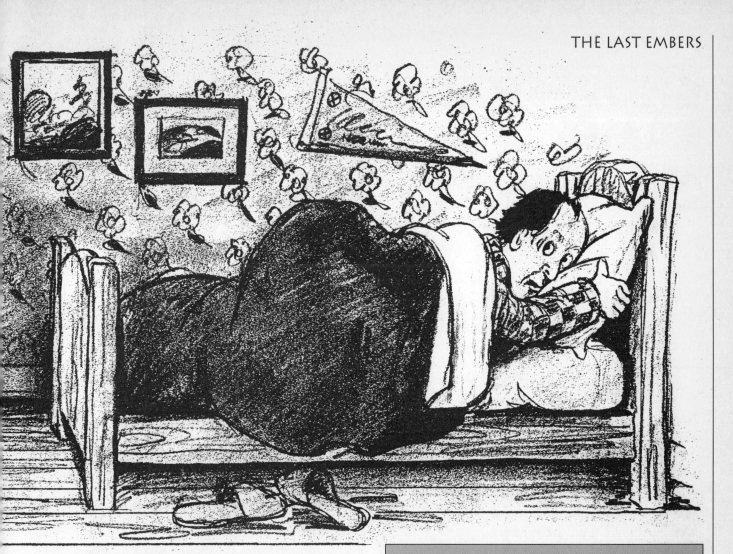

his wife's voice. "Where is my golden arm?"

The next night, he locked the front door and pushed the couch in front of it. He locked his bedroom door and pushed the chest of drawers in front of it too. In the middle of the night he woke up to a moaning that seemed to come from beside his bed. This time, he was sure it was his wife's voice. "Where is my golden arm?"

Now turn and look directly at one listener and shout — "You've got it!"

LOCAL GHOST STORIES

There may be a good ghost story about an abandoned cabin nearby, or an old hotel. Look for history books in the nearest library — there may have been an unexplained death or disappearance in pioneer times that you can weave into your spooky tale.

GHOST-STORY GAMES

After you've told a few ghost stories and are in a creepy mood, keep those goosebumps raised by playing a ghost-story game.

MURDER IN THE DARK

You play this game with three or more players — the more the better. Using a deck of cards, count out as many cards as there are players. Choose one of the cards to represent the murderer, such as the Jack of Spades. All players pick a card, look at it and replace the card in the pile. Someone shouts, "There's a murderer on the loose," and everyone scatters into the darkness beyond the fire.

The murderer hides and waits for a player to pass by. He leaps out and touches the victim and says, "Got you!" That player becomes the murderer's assistant and helps the murderer look for the rest of the players. But the murderer has to be the one to catch or touch all the others. The last person to be caught wins.

MURDER HANDSHAKE

This game is a variation on Murder in the Dark. In this game, the murderer uses a deadly handshake to catch victims.

Make up an unusual handshake for the murderer such as sliding the hand over the victim's palm or flicking the victim's wrist with one finger. The murderer is chosen by cards or by an adult choosing one murderer and whispering in all players' ears either "murderer" or "victim."

Instead of hiding, everyone wanders around shaking hands. When a player receives the murder handshake, he shakes three more people's hands and then collapses on the ground. Players can accuse others of being the murderer. If they are right, they win and start over, but if they are wrong, they lie down and play dead. Continue to play until the entire group knows who the murderer is.

FOXFIRE

Tonight, the campfire might develop an eerie glow. Is it a sign or an evil omen? It could be, but it's likely foxfire. Decaying wood can contain a luminescent (glow-in-the-dark) fungus. When it burns, the fire has a special shine called foxfire.

MURDER WINK

You can play Murder Wink while sitting in a circle around the campfire. Choose a murderer as you did in Murder Handshake. If the murderer winks at another player, that person falls over and is out of the game. Everyone tries to avoid making eye contact with the other people in the circle, but it is impossible not to sneak a peek. Once you know who the murderer is, shout his name, before he gives you a deadly wink. If you have guessed correctly, you win, but if you are wrong you're out.

OWL AND MOUSE HIDE-AND-SEEK

The object of this game is to hide safely as close to the Owl as possible, without the Owl seeing you — because you are a mouse!

Choose a home base close to the campfire but outside the glow of light. Someone is chosen to be the Owl and all the others are mice. The Owl stands at home base counting to 20 while the mice hide. The Owl can't move her feet, but after counting to 20 she can move her head around, looking for the mice. The Owl calls out the names of anyone she sees and that person is out. When the Owl can't see any more mice, she calls out "number" and holds up her hand, signaling a number between one and five. All remaining mice must look at the number, but any mice spotted trying to see her hand signal are called out too. The last person closest to the Owl, and who knows the correct number of fingers held up, wins and becomes the Owl next.

YOUR SIXTH SENSE

Your five senses are tuned into the campfire evening. You see the Sun set, hear the fire crackling, smell the smoke, touch the sticky marshmallow and taste it too. As the shadows get longer are you aware of another sense, one that tells you there is someone or some creature behind you? Your spine tingles, your heart races, you spin around — and there they are. It's probably your brother or the family cat ready to pounce.

Test people's sixth sense by hiding in the shadows and creeping up from behind. How close can you get? They won't know they're playing the game until they yell, "Oh, you scared me!"

SARDINES SEARCH

There is safety in numbers when you play this game. One person hides in a snug spot such as a shed, a hammock or under a porch while the others count out loud to 30. Players look for the hidden person by themselves, not as a group. When you find the hiding spot, quietly climb in and hide too. When everyone has jammed in like sardines in a tin, it's time to start again.

NIGHT SMELLS

As the night gets darker, you lose your sense of sight but your hearing sharpens and smells seem stronger. You can identify the pungent aroma of the nocturnal skunk, but did you know that the ermine, a member of the weasel family, also sprays a warning? Its smell is like a mild skunk. But unlike the waddling skunk, it's so quick, you'll be lucky if you ever see one.

CAMPFIRE SLEEP OUT

The fire is almost out and the night sky is clear. Why not sleep under the stars? With a little preparation, you can settle in for some interesting nightwatching and a good sleep. The bare ground is a comfortable place to sleep if you follow a few simple rules.

Even if the campfire is out, make sure your sleeping site is at least 3 m (10 ft.) from the fire pit. Ground and rock around a fire can remain hot for a long time.

Look for dry ground that is soil-covered and sprouting grass or plants. Don't lie on moss because it acts like a sponge and holds water.

Look for a smooth site without lumps and bumps such as stones, roots, branches or twigs jutting up.

A shirt stuffed with socks and jeans makes a good pillow.

Lay down a groundsheet to keep any night dampness from seeping into your sleeping bag. Good groundsheets are heavy and do not rustle when touched. A picnic table oilcloth, a tarpaulin or heavy plastic sheet are all fine, but do not use thin plastic like a dry-cleaning bag.

Lay your sleeping bag on the groundsheet so the head end is slightly above the foot end if possible. Make sure the site is flat side to side so that you won't roll. In mid to late August, lay a heavy groundsheet on top of your sleeping bag as well. Early-morning dew can dampen a pleasant morning.

Take off any underclothes and socks that you sweated in earlier in the day — you will feel chilled if you wear them in bed. Even on a cool night, no clothes are better than damp ones.

Before crawling into your sleeping bag, double-check that the fire is doused and dead.

Look around and get to know the night before you fall asleep. Good Night.

METEOR SHOWER SLEEP OUT

On any summer night, you can see three or four meteors, also called shooting stars. For several nights before and after August 12, the Perseid meteor shower is at its peak. You may see at least a dozen shooting stars every hour after dark — and more frequently after midnight — so it's a great time for a sleep out. Look for the meteors in the northeast toward Cassiopeia (see page 63).

NORTHERN LIGHTS

If you see a greenish white glow in the northern night sky, it's likely northern lights. In southern Canada and the northern U.S. this glow is seen most often in late August and September. Farther north, it is seen more regularly. Occasionally, the glow turns into a band of rays spiking up into the sky along the northern horizon. On very special nights, the band appears to develop folds and looks like a giant curtain swaying across most of the sky. Northern lights come in white, pink, red, yellow or blue and can be hundreds of kilometers (miles) long.

DOUSING THE FIRE

As the evening gets late, stop adding fuel to the fire and let it burn low. Get the most out of your fuel by pushing the coals close together. When the last marshmallow is eaten and you're being eaten by mosquitoes, it's time to douse the fire.

PUTTING OUT THE FIRE

People cause most forest fires, so make sure your fire is completely out before you say good night. You can put a fire out without water by using large quantities of sand and dirt, but it's safer to use water.

1.
Using a pail of water, sprinkle water on the coals with your fingers.

2.
Separate the coals and any wood with a poker.

3.

Slowly pour or sprinkle a pail of water on the campfire. A quick splash of lots of water doesn't work. The water will rush away from the fire site and won't douse the coals.

4.

Stir the coals again with the poker and continue to add water until the steam and smoke are completely gone.

5.

When the steam and smoke are gone, an adult should be able to run a hand through the ashes. If the ground is cold, you've doused the fire properly. Cover the ashes with soil or sand.

CAMPFIRE CLEAN

Try to make as little garbage as possible so it will be easy to keep the campfire area clean and litter free. Food scraps can attract unwanted flies and night visitors. Waste must either be burned at the site or taken with you for proper disposal or recycling. Dry burnable waste, such as paper wrappings, can be used to start fires. Wet peelings can be dried beside the fire and then burned when the cooking is finished. Dried orange peels will add a pleasant smell to the wood smoke.

CAMPFIRE SONGS

One of the best things about being around a fire is singing some familiar campfire songs. Encourage the neighbors to sing along. Maybe a loon will join in too. Learn to sing an echo song, add your own verse, do a peppy action song, sing a round or relax with a traditional campfire melody. Dust off the old guitar and add a few strums, or jazz up the sing-along with drums and other homemade instruments (see page 48).

ROUNDS

A round is a song that moves from group to group around a circle. Most rounds are short and simple, and they repeat themselves. Divide the campfire singers into two or more groups and decide which group will start. Group 1 sings the first line of the round. When they reach the end of the line (shown by this symbol ☞▯), group 2 starts the first line of the round. Group 1 sets the song's speed and mood. Soon everyone will keep up with the pace and enjoy the harmony.

FIRE'S BURNING

Fi - re's burn - ing, fi - re's burn - ing. Draw near - er, draw near - er. In the

glow - ing, in the glow - ing. Come sing and be mer - ry.

CANOE SONG

chorus
Dip, dip and swing. Dip, dip and swing. Dip, dip and swing. Dip, dip and swing.

My pad-dle's big and bright, flash-ing with sil-ver. Swift as the wild goose flies. Dip, dip and swing.

(chorus)
Dip, dip and swing her back,
flashing with silver.
Swift as the wild goose track.
Dip, dip and swing.

(repeat chorus)

98

FRÈRE JACQUES

Frè - re Ja - cques, Frè - re Ja - cques, dor - mez - vous, dor - mez - vous ?

Son-nez les ma - ti - nes, son-nez les ma - ti - nes, ding, dang, dong; ding, dang, dong.

Are you sleeping, are you sleeping,
Brother John, Brother John?
Morning bells are ringing, morning bells are ringing,
Ding, dang, dong; ding, dang, dong.

TALL TREES

Tall trees that reach the sky. Moun-tains and lakes near - by. Draw

near with friends, come sing, my friends, our camp - fire time is nigh.

LIGHT THE WOOD

G   Em   G   C   D7

Light the wood, the camp-fire burns,   we are gath-ered all a - round.

G   Em   G   C   D7   G

Now the flames are leap - ing high,   light - ing up the even - ing sky.

ECHO-AND-ANSWER SONGS

To sing echo-and-answer songs, divide the group in two. One group sings a phrase and then is echoed or answered by the other group. Each song here is a little different than the next, so follow the instructions on each page. Add fun to the song by changing your tone of voice, plugging your nose or sounding exasperated.

In this echo song, group 1 sings "There was a tree," then group 2 repeats "There was a tree," followed by group 1 singing "all in the wood" and so on. The symbol (**E**) marks the spot where group 1 pauses to hear the echo sung by group 2. Everyone sings the rest of each verse together.

THE GREEN GRASS GROWS ALL AROUND

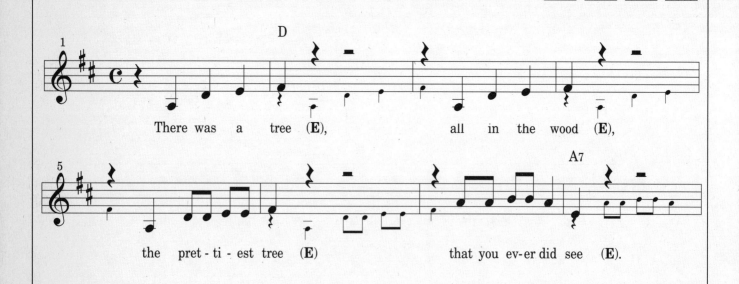

The tree in a hole and the hole in the ground, and the green grass grew all a-round, all a-round, and the green grass grew all a-round.

And on that tree (**E**) there was a limb (**E**),
the prettiest limb (**E**) that you ever did see (**E**).
The limb on the tree, and the tree in the hole,
and the green grass grew all around, all around,
and the green grass grew all around.

And on that limb (**E**) there was a branch (**E**) ...

And on that branch (**E**) there was a twig (**E**) ...

And on that twig (**E**) there was a needle (**E**) ...

103

DAISY

This is an answer song. Group 1 sings the first verse
and group 2 answers with the second.

Dai - sy, Dai - sy, give me your an - swer true,
I'm half cra - zy o - ver my love for you. It
won't be a sty - lish mar - riage, we can't af - ford a car - riage. But
you'll look sweet up - on the seat of a bi - cy - cle built for two.

Harry, Harry, here is my answer to you.
You're half crazy if you think I'd marry you.
If you can't afford a carriage,
then you can't afford our marriage.
So please retreat upon the seat
of your bicycle built for two.

MY AUNT CAME BACK

A E7 Bm

This is an echo-action song. Repeat each phrase and add one action per verse.

Oh, my aunt came back (**E**), from Hol-land too (**E**), and she brought with her (**E**) a wood-en shoe (**E**).

(stamp your foot on the word "shoe" and keep stamping)

Oh, my aunt came back (**E**)
from Old Japan (**E**),
And she brought with her (**E**)
a waving fan (**E**).
(wave a fan with one hand)

. . . from Open Plain (**E**), . . .
a walking cane (**E**).
(walk with cane)

. . . from near Kamloops (**E**), . . .
some hula hoops (**E**).
(rotate hips in a hula hoop movement)

. . . from near Algiers (**E**), . . .
some cutting shears (**E**).
(snip with hand)

. . . from New York Fair (**E**), . . .
a rocking chair (**E**).
(rock forward and back)

. . . from Niagara Falls (**E**), . . .
some Ping-Pong balls (**E**).
(throw hands in the air)

105

THERE'S A HOLE IN MY BUCKET

Divide into a "Henry" group and a "Liza" group and sing to each other. Change the tone of the song by having the "Henry" group sing in a whiny voice and the "Liza" group sing in an impatient voice.

There's a hole in my buck - et, dear Li - za, dear Li - za, there's a hole in my buck - et, dear Li - za, a hole.

Then fix it, dear Henry, dear Henry, dear Henry,
then fix it, dear Henry, dear Henry, fix it.

With what shall I fix it, dear Liza, dear Liza,
with what shall I fix it, dear Liza, with what?

With a straw . . .

But the straw is too long . . .

Then cut it . . .

With what shall I cut it? . . .

With a knife . . .

But the knife is too dull . . .

Then sharpen it . . .

With what shall I sharpen it? . . .

With a stone . . .

But the stone is too dry . . .

Then wet it . . .

With what shall I wet it? . . .

With water . . .

Well, how shall I carry it? . . .

In a bucket . . .

But there's a hole in my bucket . . .

ACTION SONGS

Action songs tell a story through words and actions. In "Cabin in the Wood" use your hands to create a little roof over your head for the cabin, indicate the man is little with your thumb and finger, then peek out the window with your imaginary binoculars, and so on. Once you've mastered all the moves you can stand up in front of the campfire group and lead them through this action song.

Try leaving out the words, one phrase at a time, and just do the action. Then sing the song again from the beginning.

CABIN IN THE WOOD

In a cab - in in the wood,
(hands over head like a roof)

little old man by the win - dow stood.
(thumb and finger held to show small, then hands around eyes like binoculars)

Saw a rab - bit hop - ping by,
(two fingers up on one hand, make bunny hop along)

fright - ened as can be.
(arms around body as if scared)

"Help me, help me," the rab - bit said,
(fling arms in air to signal help, point to self)

"or that hun - ter will shoot me dead."
(pretend to shoot gun)

"Come, lit - tle rab - bit, come with me,
(use two hands to beckon the rabbit)

hap - py we will be."
(two fingers up on one hand to form bunny, pat back of hand with other hand)

DO YOUR EARS HANG LOW?

A   E7

A

Do your ears hang low?   Do they wob-ble to and fro?   Can you
(backs of hands on ears, fingers down)   *(sway fingers)*

E7   A

tie them in a knot? Can you tie them in a bow? Can you throw them over your shoul-der Like a
(tie knot in air)   *(draw bow in air)*   *(throw hands over shoulder)*

E7   A

con-tin-en-tal sol-dier? Do your ears   hang   low?
(salute)   *(backs of hands on ears, fingers down)*

110

THE MORE WE GET TOGETHER

The more we get to - ge - ther, to - ge - ther, to - ge - ther, the

more we get to - ge - ther, the hap - pi - er we'll be. 'Cause

your friends are my friends, and my friends are your friends. The
(point to others)   *(point to self)*   *(point to self)*   *(point to others)*

more we get to - ge - ther, the hap - pi - er we'll be. Oh,
(repeat)

111

ALOUETTE AND ALOUETTESKI

A - lou - et - te, gen - tille A - lou - et - te, A - lou - et - te,

je - te plu - me - rai.

solo
Je te plu - me - rai la tête
(point to head)

chorus
Je te plu - me - rai la tête

solo
Et la tête

chorus
Et la tête

solo
A - lou - ette!

chorus
A - lou - ette! Ohhhhhhhhhh!

D. C. al Fine

Russian Style

Alouette, gentille Alouette,	Alouettski, gentille Alouettski,
Alouette, je te plumerai.	Alouettski, je te plumerai, Hey!
Je te plumerai le nez . . .	Je te plumerai la têtski
	Je te plumerai la têtski
. . . Je te plumerai le cou . . .	Et la têtski
	Et la têtski
. . . Je te plumerai le bras . . .	Alouettski!
	Alouettski!
(continue adding on another	Ohhhhhhhhhhh!
body part and pointing to it	
as follows: le dos, les genoux,	Alouettski, gentille Alouettski,
. . . etc.)	Alouettski, je te plumerai, Hey!
	Je te plumerai le nezovitch . . .

*(continue adding on another body part as follows: le
les yeuxzovitch, les kneesknockovitch . . . etc.)*

SWIMMING HOLE

G C Am7 D7

G · · · · C · · · G
Swim - ming, swim - ming in the swim-ming hole, when
(swimming strokes) *(circle with hands)*

C · · · G · · · Am7 · · · D7
days are hot, when days are cold, in the swim - ming hole.
(wipe brow) *(hug yourself)* *(circle with hands)*

G · · · · · C · · · G
Breast stroke, side stroke, fan - cy div - ing too, Oh
(imitate each stroke in turn)

C · · · G · · · G · · D7 · G
don't you wish you ne - ver had an - y-thing else to do... But
(point finger) *(back to the beginning)*

Sing once and then repeat, leaving out one phrase at a
time — just do the actions. Finish off with a loud "But!"

ADD-A-VERSE SONGS

You'll have to use your imagination for these songs. Each singer adds to the basic song by telling a joke, completing a verse or reciting a nursery rhyme. The possibilities are endless — the song ends when you run out of ideas.

114

STAY ON THE SUNNY SIDE — A JOKE SONG

Everyone sings the chorus and then each person takes a turn telling a silly joke. Here are a few suggestions to get you started.

Stay on the sun-ny side, al-ways on the sun-ny side, stay on the sun-ny side of life. You will feel no pain as we drive you in-sane, if you stay on the sun-ny side of life.

Knock, knock. Who's there?
Dwain. Dwain who?
Dwain the lake, I'm dwowning.

(chorus)

What do you call a cow with no legs?
Ground beef.

(chorus)

What's green and flies?
Super pickle.

(chorus)

Where did the vampire do his banking?
The blood bank.

(chorus)

115

DOWN BY THE BAY

chorus
Down by the bay, where the water-melons grow, Back to my home, I dare not go, for if I do, my mo-ther will say: Did you ev-er see a turtle, wear-ing a girdle? Down by the bay,

(chorus)
Did you ever see a newt, eating some fruit?
Down by the bay,

(chorus)
Did you ever see a goose, kissing a moose?
Down by the bay,

(chorus)
Did you ever see a loon, crying at the moon?
Down by the bay,

(chorus)

THE WINDOW

Divide into two groups and take turns singing a nursery rhyme. Everyone joins in with the chorus. Continue singing until you run out of rhymes.

Don't forget: Old King Cole, Little Jack Horner, Little Boy Blue, Hickory Dickory Dock …

chorus Mar - y had a lit - tle lamb, its fleece was white as snow, and

ev - ery - where that Mar - y went, she threw it out the win - dow, the

wind - ow, the wind - ow, the se - cond - sto - rey win - dow, if

you don't know your nurs - ery rhymes, we'll throw you out the win - dow.

TRADITIONAL CAMPFIRE SONGS

These songs are a must for campfire singing. You'll soon pick favorites to sing at every gathering. That's why these are called traditional songs. They've been sung around campfires for years.

HOME ON THE RANGE

Oh, give me a land where
the bright diamond sands
lie awash in the glittering stream,

where days glide along in pleasure and song,
and afternoons pass as a dream.
Home, home on the range...

BILL GROGAN'S GOAT

A   D   E7

Bill Gro - gan's goat, was feel - ing fine, ate three red

shirts, right off the line.

Bill grabbed that goat, by the wool of the back,
and he tied him to, the railroad track.

That goat he bucked, with might and main,
as round the curve, came a passenger train.

That goat he bucked, with might and main,
coughed up those shirts, and flagged the train.

120

CAMPFIRE

chorus

Ga-ther round the fire to-night, ho- la hi, ho- la ho. Let us sing with all our might, ho- la, hi- la ho. How we re - mem - ber those hap - py days, ho - la hi, ho - la ho. Spent in the light of the camp - fire blaze, ho- la, hi- la ho.

FOUND A PEANUT

Found a pea - nut, found a pea - nut, found a pea - nut, la - st night.

La - st night I found a pea - nut, found a pea - nut, la - st night.

Broke it open, broke it open,
broke it open, last night.
Last night I broke it open,
broke it open, last night.

It was rotten . . .

Ate it anyway . . .

Got a stomach ache . . .

Called the doctor . . .

Penicillin . . .

Operation . . .

Died anyway . . .

Went to heaven . . .

Wouldn't take me . . .

Went the other way . . .

Didn't want me . . .

It was a dream . . .

Woke up . . .

Found a peanut . . .

BOOM BOOM
(AIN'T IT GREAT TO BE CRAZY)

A horse and a flea and three blind mice sat on a curb-stone shoot-ing dice. The

horse he slipped and fell on the flea. "Oops," said the flea, "there's a horsey on me." Boom,

boom, ain't it great to be cra - zy, boom, boom, ain't it great to be cra - zy.

Gid - dy and fool - ish all day long. Boom, boom, ain't it great to be cra - zy.

Eli, Eli, he sells socks,
five cents a pair or a dollar a box.
The longer you wear them, the shorter they get.
You put them in the water and they don't get wet.
(chorus)

123

MMM LINGER

Mm - m, I want to lin - ger. Mm - m, a lit - tle

long - er. Mm - m, a lit - tle long - er here with you.

Mmm, it's such a perfect night.
Mmm, it doesn't seem quite right.
Mmm, that this should be our last with you.

Mmm, and so as the years go by.
Mmm, we'll think of you and sigh.
Mmm, this is goodnight and not goodbye.

(repeat the first verse)

TAPS

Day is done, gone the sun, from the lakes, from the hills, from the

sky, all is well, safe - ly rest, peace is nigh.

SONGS

INDEX OF TITLES

INDEX OF FIRST LINES

INDEX